A L L

E L S E

E Q U A L

A L L
E L S E
E Q U A L

Are Public and Private Schools Different?

By Luis Benveniste,
Martin Carnoy,
and Richard Rothstein

 RoutledgeFalmer
Taylor & Francis Group

NEW YORK AND LONDON

Published in 2003 by
RoutledgeFalmer
29 West 35th Street
New York, NY 10001
www.routledge-ny.com

Published in Great Britain by
RoutledgeFalmer
11 New Fetter Lane
London EC4P 4EE
www.routledgefalmer.com

10 9 8 7 6 5 4 3 2 1

Library of Congress Cataloging-in-Publication Data

Benveniste, Luis.
   All else equal : are public and private schools different? / by Luis Benveniste, Martin Carnoy, and Richard Rothstein.
      p. cm.
   Includes bibliographical references.
   ISBN 0-415-93196-7 (alk. paper) — ISBN 0-415-93197-5 (pbk. : alk. paper)
      1. Privatization in education—United States. 2. Public schools—United States—California—Case studies. 3. Private schools—United States—California—Case studies. I. Carnoy, Martin. II. Benveniste, Luis. III. Title.

   LB2806.36 .R68 2002
   371.01'0973—dc21
                                                         2002026714

CONTENTS

Acknowledgments

This book is based on and is an expansion of an earlier book by the authors, *Can Public Schools Learn From Private Schools?*, published in 1999 by the Economic Policy Institute and co-published by The Aspen Institute's Nonprofit Sector Research Fund. Research for this book was supported by the Aspen Institute's Nonprofit Sector Research Fund, the Consortium for Policy Research in Education, the Economic Policy Institute, and the U.S. Department of Education—Office of Educational Research and Improvement (Grant No. OERI-R308A60003).

We are indebted to Zoe Gillett, Matt Kelemen, Paula Louzano, Jennifer O'Day, Diana Rhoten, Gayatri Sethi, and Sandra Stein for their contributions in the school case studies upon which the field research of this book is based. Their thoughtful insights inspired and nourished much of our thinking.

We are also deeply grateful to the principals, teachers, parents, students, and administrators that welcomed us into their schools and kindly shared their experiences and points of view with us. We were immensely enriched by their frank comments and perceptive observations.

This book reflects our own views of the nature and conditions of private and public schooling. The findings, analyses, and conclusions expressed in this study are entirely those of the authors.

PREFACE

Americans' perceptions of public and private schools may be changing. Is this mainly a result of a new reality or a misreading of complex educational data? Certainly, public schooling has been discredited in the past generation, attacked as dominated by bureaucratic rules and rigid labor unions, blind to the interests of children and parents, and laced with violence and immorality. Some analysts have advocated private schooling as an efficient, competitive antidote to this failing public education system. Others have found a model to emulate in urban Catholic education, transformed by economic necessity to serve a more non-Catholic, minority constituency and so fitting the "common school" ideal more so than public schools. Many political and community leaders advocate direct public financing of religious and nonreligious private education.

Critics claim that public schools are failing to meet social goals, so America needs private schooling, especially for urban low-income populations, to restore economic mobility and to preserve American values. At the least, some of these critics of public education argue that the more that private schools are made available as an alternative, the more efficiently the educational system as a whole will perform.

Are the attacks on public schooling and the push to privatize it justified? Many policymakers are convinced that private education is really better and cheaper than public education. It may be that, because a private school is private, it can organize itself in ways that deliver more learning. It would make sense to finance private education with public funds if that were indeed the case, especially if private schools could also provide the kind of social integration that we ask public schools to accomplish.

Researchers on both sides of the private versus public school debate have been engaged in a battle of numbers. Advocates of privatization have long mainly relied on research studies claiming that private secondary schools are academically superior to public high schools and that this proves that a competitive education market would make major improvements in American education.

However, when the results are studied carefully, they turn out to be mixed and often conflicting. Researchers rightly try to correct for students' family background when measuring the effect of classroom and school characteristics on student performance. They want to estimate how much teachers and the school environment contribute over and above the contribution of family environment or particular race or ethnic community conditions. But beyond characteristics like race, ethnicity, parents' education, free-lunch eligibility, or articles in the home, researchers have relatively little information on family inputs into childrens' academic performance. This is particularly important when it comes to comparing the performance of children in public and private schools, because parents' choices of schools may imply difficult to measure beliefs about the importance of education that can affect achievement.

Once the social background of children attending different schools, as measured by the characteristics for which data are available, is accounted for, some evidence suggests that private education produces higher achievement and attainment than does public. But other, equally compelling evidence suggests that students from similar backgrounds make about the same achievement gains whether they attend private or public schools.

Thus, after several decades of discussion, we still need to answer some hard questions. Are private schools really better educational institutions? Do they do things differently from public schools? Does a market in education, in which private schools compete with public schools and with each other, make for better teaching, more parent participation, and higher student achievement?

We have been exploring these questions and will report on some of our findings in this book. In the following pages, we trace the genealogy of intellectual arguments for private education, present some of the criticisms made of these arguments, and review the empirical studies on private–public school differences. Yet the main contribution we make to answering the question of whether private schools are really "better" than public schools is to examine the issue firsthand, by going to the schools. We report on interviews with teachers, parents, and administrators in sixteen public and private elementary and middle schools in California.* We did not select a random sample of schools. Instead, we focused on different kinds of institutions to get a sense of the variety of situations in the world of education. As we went from school to school, we searched for patterns. One main pattern that we looked for were those systematic differences between private and public schools touted by many policy analysts and proponents of education markets.

Because private schools can select (and are selected by) their students, analysts have not been able to determine whether private schools' apparently superior outcomes (like test scores) are attributable to superior private school practices or to more selective stu-

---

* We did not include secondary schools in our analysis, although we did conduct interviews in several private and public secondary schools. Thus, we do not cover in this book the same level of schooling as do the many studies comparing public and private secondary school cohorts of the early 1980s and 1990s.

dent bodies. Some studies finding that private school students do better than public school students may be the result of self-selection among lower–social class parents who opt to send their children to private rather than to public school—the children of more highly motivated parents who choose private schools will likely do better than other children, whether they go to public or private schools. Yet there may be organizational and curricular reasons for the higher achievement and attainment of private school pupils.

To the extent that private school practices are responsible, these practices are widely believed to include more accountability to parents, more clearly defined outcome expectations, a greater clarity of emphasis on both academic and behavioral and value objectives, and more efficient teacher selection and retention policies. Private schools mostly utilize the same curricular materials as public schools, and so private schools' apparently superior outcomes should be able to inspire competing public schools to improve by imitating private school practices.

In our case studies of eight public and eight private schools in California, we conducted extensive interviews with principals, other administrators, teachers, parents, and (in the case of some eighth graders) students. The schools were selected to typify a range of socioeconomic characteristics and included both sectarian and nonsectarian private schools. However, we make no claim that the sample of schools was scientifically chosen or that the impressions we record here are statistically valid. The depth with which we probed each of these schools precluded a large enough sample to generate statistical conclusions.

To our surprise, we found few of the differences that we expected to find between public and private schools in similar communities. Upon reflection, we do not think this finding resulted from having too small a sample and believe that our findings are of broader significance. The claim of market theorists, after all, is that market-driven behavior is observably and significantly different from the bureaucratically driven behavior characteristic of public schools. If this were the case, at least some significant differences ought to be observable in a sample of eight public and eight private schools. If they are not at all observable in our small but very carefully studied sample, then it is puzzling to imagine what contrary characteristics a larger sample would reveal.

As we report in this book, insights from these case studies tend to challenge widely held assumptions about differences between public and private schools. Inner-city private schools shared more characteristics with public schools in low-income communities than with affluent suburban private schools. Likewise, suburban public schools had more in common with suburban private schools than with urban public schools. Thus, policy debates about education may be missing the most important issues if they focus on whether a school's quality can be deduced from its public or private charter. The most important variations between schools may be between schools of all types in different communities, not between public and private schools in the same community.

Among the sixteen schools in this sample, private schools were not noticeably more accountable to parents than public schools. In low-income schools, public and private, teachers and administrators complained of the lack of parental involvement. Both public and private schoolteachers in these low-income communities felt challenged to involve parents even in a minimal way in their children's education (e.g., by supervising homework or attending school meetings). And in no sense did we observe either public or private schools in low-income communities acting as though they were "accountable" to parents. But an opposite phenomenon characterized both public and private schools in very affluent communities: here, staff in both types of schools complained of *too much* parent involvement, including interference in the daily curriculum and inappropriate challenges to school goals.

Policymakers often posit that private schools are more successfully organized around academic achievement objectives and are more successful in emphasizing behavioral goals. These case studies, however, include private schools organized around principles other than academic outcomes, such as religious beliefs, safety, or discipline; in some cases, academic achievement was a relatively low priority. The studies also found some public schools that were as successful as private ones in aligning themselves with academic goals and some public schools that also emphasized behavioral or value objectives.

Many believe that an important public–private difference is the laxity of teacher standards stimulated by public employee protections and unionization. Yet these case studies found no school, public or private, where formal evaluation, supervision, or mentoring of teachers were meaningful. Indeed, Catholic school procedures for terminating poorly performing teachers were nearly as cumbersome as public school procedures. Moreover, private schools in this sample were no more selective in teacher personnel policies than were public schools serving students of similar socioeconomic backgrounds. We observed both high- and low-quality classroom management and academic instruction in both public and private schools.

The social, cultural, and economic backgrounds of the parents and the community in which the school was located seemed to be the main determinant of variation, much more so than a school's public or private character or, within the latter group, whether it was religious or secular. Within particular communities, similarities between schools and the problems that they confronted overwhelmed the differences.

Most theoretical arguments about public and private education, advanced by advocates of privatization, conclude that a free market in schools should increase the variety of education models and the choices open to parents. Our findings, that private schools and public schools offer very similar models to parents of similar socioeconomic circumstances, may seem, therefore, to be without theoretical basis.

However, there is a competing theory, less widely repeated than free-market arguments, that explains our findings nicely. An economist, Byron Brown, predicted in 1992 that private and public schools would not differ significantly. Because parents are generally uncertain about children's abilities and future employment prospects, Professor Brown argued, public and private schools trying to appeal to parents all offer comprehensive curricula and similar teaching methods in order to reduce the uncertainty about schooling choices. If a school chooses to differ radically from other schools, it increases the risk to parents that they have made the wrong choice. Whether by voice or exit, parents will push the school that their child attends to behave much like other schools. Brown concluded that private schools will not tend to distinguish themselves by innovating academically. His argument is consistent with what we have found.

Our sixteen case studies of public and private schools point away from arguments that public schools can improve by adopting greater accountability to parents and flexibility in the hiring and firing of teachers, presumably characteristics of private schools. These may be good policies for all schools to follow, but public schools are as likely (or unlikely) to be accountable to parents as private schools serving similar student and parent populations. These observations, if confirmed by observations of a much broader group of schools, could have important implications for those who champion choice in public education as the basis for improving academic achievement. A much greater complexity of factors must be considered when developing "fixes" for our nation's schools.

ALL

ELSE

EQUAL

[1]

RECASTING PUBLIC AND PRIVATE EDUCATION IN POSTINDUSTRIAL AMERICA

The attacks on public education and the promotion of private education do not appear to reflect any discernible shift in where Americans actually send their children to school. For tens of millions of European immigrants in the nineteenth and early twentieth centuries, public schools served as a bridge to assimilation. For the Civil Rights movement, desegregating public schools was crucial to achieving greater equality. So, today, the new wave of immigrants after 1970, this time from Latin America and Asia, is enrolled almost entirely in public schools.

Indeed, public schools continue to be the mainstay of American education, with approximately 90 percent of all children in public kindergarten to twelfth grade (U.S. Department of Education, 1999). This overall percentage has not varied much in the second half of the twentieth century. Private school enrollment may have reached its highest point in 1965 when more than 6 million children (5.5 million in Catholic schools), took private education. This represented 11 percent of the total U.S. elementary and high school enrollment. At the end of the 1990s, there may actually have been fewer children in private school than 35 years ago, both in absolute and relative terms. Since average real family income rose substantially in the period, the lack of significant movement into private education is surprising.[1]

The number of children attending private schools may not have increased, but the configuration of private schooling itself has changed drastically since the mid-1960s. Then, 90 percent of private school students were in Catholic schools located mainly in the urban centers of the Northeast and Great Lakes regions. In a society dominated by Protestant values and political power, Catholic education represented an important alternative to secular education for European immigrant communities rooted in Catholicism and ethnic identity—first the Irish, then the Italians and Polish. As these groups produced their own elites, Catholic preparatory schools began to do for Catholics what New England academies did for Protestants. But when white ethnic minorities moved to the suburbs, they were assimilated into the broad, public school-going middle class. By the late 1990s, only 50 percent of private education students attended Catholic schools, and new denominations of non-Catholic religious schools had spread to the suburban and rural areas of the South and West. In the South of the 1970s, part of this change was connected to school integration and white flight from public schools. By the 1980s, the growth of non-Catholic religious schools, particularly Evangelical Christian schools, was a nationwide phenomenon (Cooper, 1988).

During the past few decades, the public school system has come under fire. There has been a growing concern over violence, poor funding for educational programs, and low student achievement in our nation's schools. Yet an important distinction must be drawn about this overall picture. While Americans have traditionally expressed dissatisfaction with the conditions of public schooling *in generic terms,* they have historically given high praise to those schools in their communities. As a recent annual poll conducted by *Phi Delta Kappa/Gallup* demonstrates, a majority of respondents (51 percent of the general population and 62 percent of public school parents) assigned a grade of either A or B to their local public school, reaching a record high in the poll's 33-year history (Rose and Gallup, 2001).

Although most Americans do not agree that their childrens' public schools are selling them short, many low-income African Americans and Latinos living in America's cities look at it differently (Bositis, 1999). According to David Bositis, a senior political analyst at the Joint Center for Political and Economic Studies, a significantly higher proportion of blacks than whites support vouchers. This is especially true for blacks under 50 years old. But, as Bositis sees it, "black support for vouchers is mainly a rejection of the status quo— that is, poorly performing schools and students—rather than an endorsement of this particular program" (Bositis, 2001, p. A27). Blacks and Hispanics perceive that inner-city public education does not match up to suburban schools. Whether the "value added" in inner-city schools is actually lower than in suburban schools, it appears to inner-city parents that their schools do not provide the same level of services. The ideal of an efficient, innovative local school responsive to parents and dedicated to high achievement and low costs sounds to many of them just like the ticket to a suburban quality education in the heart of the inner city. Like the urban ethnic white minorities of an earlier time, who had their private alternatives to Protestant-dominated public education, some minorities seek private, African-American, Chinese, or other ethnic schools.

Today, most advocates of expanding the private school sector, and contracting the public, claim to do so in the interest of low-income, minority children. But the movement to privatize education in the United States did not begin as a program intended to benefit disadvantaged children specifically. Rather, it began a half-century ago, with a proposal by Milton Friedman to make education more efficient and less costly.

DECONSTRUCTING PUBLIC SCHOOLING
RESURRECTING THE MARKET IDEAL

Milton Friedman was barely 40 years old in the mid-1950s. He had already published the history of monetary theory that would earn him the Nobel Prize 20 years later. When Dwight Eisenhower was elected in 1952 as a moderate Republican, it was the first chance since the Depression that conservatives had to shape economic policy. Theories that relied on government intervention in and regulation of markets still dominated economic thinking in the 1950s, yet Friedman and others, who believed in markets as self-regulators and carried a deep distrust of government intervention in the economy, became influential.

Their influence extended to social policy, for which the Eisenhower administration was generally supportive of more conservative approaches. By the late 1940s, Friedman had already moved outside his specialty in macroeconomic policy to test his ideas on labor markets and other more micro aspects of public issues. Now he extended these ideas to social issues. His model was simple. Whatever public intervention or government regulation Friedman was interested in, he would show that it made things worse for society than would a freely operating market. Yet, in an era when the G.I. bill was sending tens of thousands of young men to college at government expense, when rising government employment was beginning to help women and black professionals attain middle-class incomes, and when Social Security was reducing poverty in the older population, Friedman's ideas about government and markets were hardly mainstream.

Friedman's essay on education first appeared in a collection edited by Robert Solo in 1955 (Friedman, 1955). In it, Friedman made two simple arguments against the public education system. By assigning pupils to public schools based on neighborhood residency, the system restricted freedom of choice. Families had to change where they lived in order to buy better education for their children. *Better* education not only meant higher-quality tradi-tional schooling, but also different types of schooling—more or less structured, more or less emphasis on one subject or another, and so forth. Those who could not afford to move or did not wish to move for other reasons, were forced to "buy" education that they did not want. This was also true for families sending their children to private schools to avoid unwanted public education, because these families still paid taxes for their neighborhood public school. Limits on choice reduced families' sense of well-being. Even though some families would feel satisfied with their children's neighbor-hood public school no matter what the choices, all families would be better off if government allowed them to use their tax dollars to select among educational alternatives. Some would send their chil-dren to the designated neighborhood school, but others would send them to alternative providers. No family would be worse off, but many would be better off.

Friedman's second argument spoke to education's supply side. As a monopoly, the public education system did not have to compete, and it could therefore pass inefficiencies on to the taxpayer. If school districts were unable to deliver high-quality educational services at a reasonable price, they demanded more taxes; if they were constrained by property values to deliver edu-cation at lower cost, they reduced quality. There was no incen-tive to be efficient because no competitors challenged the quality/ price ratios claimed by the local public schools. Allowing alterna-tive educational providers to compete for tax dollars would bring schools into local neighborhoods, offering better education for the same price. As families moved their children to these more efficient schools, public schools would have to figure out how to deliver bet-ter quality or lose all their students. Again, everyone would be better off.

Achieving greater choice and more competition only required a simple change in educational financing. Instead of sending tax dollars directly to schools and assigning children who lived in the neighborhood or the district to particular schools, Friedman suggested attaching an equal publicly funded allotment to each child, called a *voucher*, that could only be used to buy schooling. The voucher could be used at any school, either private or public.

Friedman's voucher plan was both simple and elegantly argued, which made it attractive and durable, especially to readers already convinced that government bureaucracy could not deliver services of any kind efficiently. Although he never claimed that private schools were capable of producing higher-quality education than public schools, this was an interpretation of his plan that grew in importance over the years. Friedman himself continued to push the idea that the *same* quality schooling could be delivered at a much lower price than was implicit in the cost of public education. In the California voucher initiatives of 1993 and 2000, proponents used the Friedman notion that the voucher amount should be about one-half the prevailing public school cost per pupil. In the Milwaukee and Cleveland voucher experiments, vouchers were initially set by the state legislatures at $2,500, again about one-half the spending per pupil in public schools. The idea that private schooling was so much more cost-efficient than public became a fundamental tenet of the new ideology entering the educational debate.

A generation later, Chris Whittle, a successful media entrepreneur, also bought Friedman's idea, or at least a modified version of it. Whittle raised considerable investment capital to develop a chain of private Edison schools that would, he claimed, be more innovative and of higher quality than public schools. He also claimed that he could accomplish this at the average cost per pupil of public schooling ($6,400 averaged across all U.S. states in 1993). Edison schools were slated to take students from preschool to eighth grade, thus avoiding the much higher costs of high schools. Even so, it is telling that Whittle was not able to launch his chain of private schools. His proposal collapsed, mainly because the schools would not have broken even financially at his promised price. Instead, he converted Edison into a management company that runs public schools. More about Edison as a private manager later.

The other pillar of Friedman's argument altering the nature of the educational debate was the beneficial effect of parental choice. Most parents already had a choice. They could move to the suburbs and they did, en masse, in the generation after Friedman's paper appeared. Blacks could also move out of the South, which they continued to do in the 1950s and 1960s, until desegregation and billions of defense dollars pouring into southern states made the South a more attractive place for blacks to work, live, and send their children to school. So Americans made many location choices, and a fair percentage of these choices included moving to places with the kind of schools that they wanted for their children. When parents made choices beyond improving economic opportunity, such as moving to the suburbs, this usually meant choosing localities with the kinds of children that they wanted their children to go to school, more than with anything particular about the quality of the schools themselves. This is quite rational. Families believe that the kinds of children who attend a school affect their child's behavior and academic performance—social scientists call this the *peer effect,* and it is far easier for parents to observe who attends a school than how effective teachers are in imparting academic skills.

But Friedman argued for expanding the available alternatives so that parents could make educational choices without moving. He went further, arguing that even allowing choices among public schools was not sufficient. This would not provide the variety of alternatives needed, because all public schools would be regulated to supply essentially the same educational product at the same cost. For Friedman, only access to private, unregulated schools at public expense would give parents meaningful alternatives to government-defined education.

Friedman, however, did not consider that, given a more extensive system of parent choice, many private and even some public schools would also have a choice. They might refuse to accept some students who applied. The market for schooling is far more complicated than the market for other goods, even health services. The ultimate outcome in education not only depends on what occurs in the classroom, but also on what occurs at home before the child enters the school, as well as on what takes place at home and among peers before and after school hours. If schools can select their students—and it is difficult to prevent them from doing so when choice rather than assignment determines who goes to a certain school—they will try to select those children who are most likely to do well academically, no matter where they attend. Given a choice, schools in central cities will try to select the "lowest-cost" students, even if their applicant pool is mostly from very low income families with few educational resources in the home. They will try to assemble a set of students that makes the school comparatively more attractive to parents seeking a good learning environment for their children.

Many proposals, such as lotteries, exist to guarantee random access to desirable schools for students and their families. But these plans often bear mixed results for a variety of reasons. Despite efforts to overcome inequalities in educational access, research on school choice suggests that it may have a stratifying effect. For instance, Lee, Croninger, and Smith (1996) report in their study of the Detroit metropolitan area that parents who expressed a preference for school choice were more likely to be wealthier and better educated than those who expressed no opinion. Evidence from voucher programs specifically targeted to the neediest sectors of the population also shows that parents who chose to enroll their children in private schools had more years of education and were more involved in their children's schooling than those who opted not to participate (Witte, 1996). This was also found to hold true in public school choice programs, such as magnet or charter schools (Martinez, Godwin, and Kemerer, 1996). Race and ethnicity considerations, as opposed to academic quality and student achievement, can play an important role as school selection criteria. A study of Montgomery County magnet schools in Maryland reveals that white families were more inclined to transfer their children into schools with low minority enrollments in higher-income neighborhoods; on the other hand, minority families sought to select schools with higher minority enrollments more characteristic of lower-income localities (Henig, 1996). Even in states that mandate ethnic or racial balances in student enrollments, such as California, choice schools tended to enroll significantly more white students than other public schools in their sponsoring district (Cobb and Glass, 2001).

Because everyone is required to attend some school up to a minimum age, this means that choice by parents could potentially lead to an even more unequal distribution of students by academic abilities than under a neighborhood assignment system. Friedman did not discuss this possibility. Implicitly, however, his analysis suggests that, if there were negative peer effect on students at the bottom of the distribution, it would be offset by greater efficiency in the educational system as a whole. Even the least desirable pupil left behind in the poorest-performing public schools would be better off, because the overall system had become so much more effective in producing more learning for all students due to increased competition. Furthermore, very bad schools would lose all their students and go out of business, making it less likely that any students would be in such learning environments.

Friedman's implicit trickle-down theory of educational quality corresponds to the efficiency–equity discussions around income inequality and economic growth. In these discussions, analysts readily admit that deregulating markets (or the existence of markets) may increase wage and income inequality. But the payoff to deregulation (or replacing a command economy with a market economy) is in raising the efficiency of production. Efficiency gains would be so great that even those with low wages would find themselves better off than in a highly regulated (and more equal income distribution) situation. A prime example of this argument is the comparison of a country such as Cuba under a totally regulated communist command economy with a Western European or free-market Latin American economy. Income distribution is much more equal in Cuba, but people have almost nothing to buy. Is it better to be a low-income family in Cuba or in Chile? In Cuba you feel much more equal with others, but your prospects for the future are grim. In Chile, you may envy the rich, but you can expect that someday you will be driving your own car. Friedman argues implicitly that, with a voucher plan and educational competition, pupils in inner-city public schools, even if they represent the lowest rung on the educational quality ladder, would be better off than in the present "command" public educational system.

ALTERNATIVES TO THE UNDEMOCRATIC STATE

Ten years later, sociologist Christopher Jencks, coming from a different political perspective, resurrected Friedman's core notion of publicly financed school choice (Jencks, 1966). The Eisenhower administration was gone, replaced by John Kennedy and the liberal (and Keynesian) Harvard crowd, and later by Lyndon Johnson, also a New Dealer. The belief in social engineering had reached its apogee in the 1960s and so had demands from social movements for major government intervention to correct discrimination and poverty. The government had responded. But in one of those fateful tricks of history, just when the liberal interventionist model should have begun to ride a crest of success, it made a major mistake—Vietnam. Opposition to the war turned liberal intellectuals and part of the Civil Rights movement openly against the state. They pushed for a more localized and humanized meaning of *public* and *private* (Carnoy and Shearer, 1980).

Like Friedman, Jencks had his doubts about what educational historian David Tyack called the "one best system" of public education (Tyack, 1974). But Jencks's concerns had different origins. Friedman elicited a profound faith in the market as an efficient and fair alternative to an overblown bureaucratic state. Jencks saw the state as an expression of a highly unequal distribution of power with roots in the market economy itself. Friedman saw the problems of public education as generalized to society as a whole. Jencks saw them as an issue primarily in poor neighborhoods, where families had to send their children to underfunded, lifeless schools. The problems of public education in these neighborhoods were an outcome of power relations that left working-class and poor parents with little access either to public or private resources, and with even less access to decision making in their schools. Jencks had no faith that within such a structure of power the needed funding to equalize opportunity for the poor would be forthcoming. The alternative was not to replace the state's control of the educational system with a generalized educational market. Jencks argued that traditional private schools *in low-income neighborhoods* might provide better schooling than did the existing public bureaucracy. But so would public and private schools controlled by parents and/or teachers (like many of today's charter schools), local universities running public schools, and city-wide public schools that would compete with each other for students.

As Jencks told us recently, "I was more concerned with creating a market for different educational approaches within public education than relying on private education to compete with public schools. I liked the idea of worker control in the private sector. Why not 'worker control' of public schools?"

The voucher plan to achieve these goals was very different from what Milton Friedman had in mind. Friedman thought that vouchers would require fewer public resources for education. Jencks began from a premise that far more (compensatory) resources were needed in education, explicitly for the poor. Friedman's voucher plan was meant to include all families. Jencks was concerned with breaking monopoly control over educational approaches mainly for low-income families, those that were cornered into sending their children to low-performing, badly organized public schools. Friedman posited that the invisible, automatic hand of the free market would make the educational system efficient and consumers better off. Jencks thought that educational competition would make education better for the poor, but he was counting more on public alternatives (public schools run by parents' and teachers; city-wide, autonomous public schools, as opposed to highly bureaucratized urban school districts) than on profit-making private schools. Jencks's vouchers were, like Friedman's, a means to break up the power over urban education held by large school bureaucracies. But Jencks's vouchers explicitly shifted financial and administrative power to a variety of communities, guided by both market forces and by community interests enforced by government regulations.

When the Nixon administration decided to develop a series of experiments in educational *performance contracting* in the early 1970s, one of the experiments chosen was vouchers. A Jencks-headed team at Harvard, including Judith Areen, David Cohen, James Breeden, David Kirp, and Marshall Smith, who later became Deputy Secretary of Education in the Clinton Administration, was given the Office of Economic Opportunity (OEO) contract to develop a voucher design that could be tested at the school district level (Center for the Study of Public Policy, 1970).

Marshall Smith reflected with us about his work with the OEO project.

> Most of the [urban] schools were a mess; they had been a mess forever. At the same time, private schools like the Roxbury Free School [in Boston's inner-city, predominantly black neighborhood] had broken out and were making real gains. They weren't representative—they involved people we

knew, graduate students and faculty members, the fruit of the loom—and there were other schools like that, but this was our example, staring us in the face. So the idea was to set up a model within a [school] district that would stimulate these kinds of schools.

But the Harvard team explicitly rejected the idea that government would not be involved—that the market would by itself produce optimal educational results. The plan (tried out in the Alum Rock school district in San Jose, California) included a provision that a certain portion of admissions would be made by lottery in oversubscribed schools to give disadvantaged students near such schools a fair choice. It also foresaw that low-income parents needed an information provision built into vouchers and that some government entity would need to provide this information. "We had templates developed of the kind of information parents needed," Smith says. "There was also no accountability system at that time, so parents needed information on how the voucher schools were performing and what exactly they were doing educationally with the children."

The voucher was explicitly compensatory. It began at an amount equal to the cost per pupil in public schools and built up from there. Lower-income pupils received more, special-education pupils even more. The plan rejected any notion that vouchers would lower schooling costs. Yet Jencks and his group did not address the question of why a society that had consistently refused to confront the issues of poverty and discrimination in a systematic way for at least two centuries would allocate more educational resources per child to poor families than to middle-class families. True, in the 2 years before 1966, Congress had passed revolutionary legislation around civil rights and the War on Poverty. But Jencks was already pessimistic in 1966 that this could translate into more educational resources for low-income families. By 1970, the War on Poverty was essentially over, and the backlash against the Civil Rights movement was already beginning.

What remained was Jencks's and other liberal thinkers' vision of low-income communities having more say about their children's schooling through greater choice among innovative and varied educational alternatives, such as the Roxbury School in Boston or the Adams Morgan School in Washington, D.C. (founded by Jencks and others in the mid-1960s). The sense that the state would not solve the problem of poor education in low-income communities also remained. This vision carried forward into the 1980s and eventually was captured by a new generation of free-market advocates in the 1990s.

THE NEW EMPIRICISM AND CATHOLIC SCHOOLING

In the interim, the National Center for Educational Statistics undertook two major longitudinal surveys, the National Longitudinal Survey of the high school senior class of 1972 and the High School and Beyond (HS&B) survey of the senior and sophomore classes of 1980. These data, especially HS&B, provided a wealth of information on high school students and their post–high school education, work experience, and income. In the early 1980s, the Department of Education commissioned several major studies as a way to stimulate use of the HS&B data. James Coleman, the author of a famous study in the mid-1960s analyzing the effects of schooling and family background on white and black academic achievement (Coleman et al., 1966), took on the project of using HS&B data to estimate student performance in private and public high schools.

Coleman's results in the 1960s were highly controversial. He presented two major findings. First, he found that socioeconomic background differences, not school facilities and resources, explained most of the variation in pupils' academic performance. Second, he found that black students who attended predominantly white schools did significantly better than blacks who went to mainly black schools.

However, in the years after his report appeared (in 1966), several re-analyses of the data found that he had underestimated the impact of schooling on academic outcomes. Samuel Bowles and Henry M. Levin (Bowles and Levin, 1968) and Eric Hanushek and John Kain (Hanushek and Kain, 1972) showed that school quality and student social background were highly correlated, so Coleman had overestimated the effect of social background on academic achievement and underestimated the effect of school quality. Schooling made more difference than Coleman had reported. Yet, as is always the case with such high-profile studies, the initial results were the ones that stuck in people's minds. Later critiques did little to change the Coleman outcome that "schools made little difference."

Looking back, Coleman may not have been right, but he was also not wrong. Students growing up in poverty face enormous barriers to doing well academically. This point is one that many Americans preferred not to face, and Coleman was not averse to making it. In the 1960s, he found sympathetic listeners inside and outside government. Solve the poverty problem, the segregation problem, and you go a long way to solving the education problem. Put young people from low-income backgrounds in schools with higher–social background students and the poorer students' performance improves significantly. Move young people from low- to higher-income neighborhoods and their academic lives also change.

Coleman was not satisfied with the result. He would have liked to show that schools do make a difference (Coleman and Hoffer, 1987). Perhaps he was concerned with what people remembered about his study or that he had failed to see what more careful analysis of the data actually demonstrated. Coleman, as sociometrician, could have been more sensitive in the 1960s to the fact that it is difficult to disentangle school effects from student socioeconomic background effects. Later studies in the 1990s demonstrated statistically that not only do higher socioeconomic background families send their children to better equipped schools, but that better teachers are also likely to choose such schools as well (Loeb and Page, 1998). And such schools are better in part because better-performing students and their parents have a positive effect on the academic atmosphere in the school (Anyon, 1983) and on their peers (see Rumberger, 1996). Some call this an expectations effect (Levin, 1998), but, whatever it is called, a conjuncture of resource and environmental conditions in schools with higher–socioeconomic background students tends to produce a very different academic experience than in schools attended by low-income students.

In the early 1980s, the HS&B data provided the vehicle for showing that schools could make an impact and, as Coleman argued later, helped him to resolve inner conflicts about the balance between his beliefs about school choice and social equity (Coleman, 1990). Coleman's estimates of private–public high school differences would present evidentiary support that schools can and do matter in shaping student outcomes (Coleman, Hoffer, and Kilgore, 1982). Because most students attending private high schools in the early 1980s were in Catholic schools and because the HS&B sampling of non-Catholic private schools was problematic, Coleman's analysis focused on differences between *Catholic* and public school achievement scores. In addition to surveying the 1980s senior class, High School and Beyond followed 1980 high school sophomores through their senior year in 1982. The survey tested both high school seniors (twelfth grade) and sophomores (tenth grade) in 1980 and the high school sophomores again in their senior year in 1982. But at the time that Coleman, Hoffer, and Kilgore did their analysis, data were available on tenth grade test scores for sophomores and twelfth grade test scores for seniors, but not the twelfth grade tests scores for 1980 sophomores. Coleman and coauthors could therefore only measure student achievement at one point in time. They did not have the test scores for the same students at two points in time, so they could not compare the *gain* in achievement by students in Catholic and public schools during the last 2 years of high school. Coleman could only answer the question of how much better seniors in 1980 did on various tests (mathematics, reading, vocabulary, writing, and science) than a different group of students in their sophomore year, also in 1980, controlling for socioeconomic background, race, ethnicity, and gender. He could also approach the question of whether students in private high schools did better than students in public schools. But he could not answer the question of whether students in Catholic schools made larger gains in achievement than students in public schools.

Coleman, Hoffer, and Kilgore argued that students in Catholic schools did significantly better. In brief, they found that, when controlling for socioeconomic background differences, sophomore and seniors in Catholic schools scored higher than in public schools. They also showed that when they compared identical subtests taken by seniors and sophomores in the same year (1980) the senior–sophomore differences for those who attended Catholic high schools were greater than the differences for students in public schools (Coleman et al., 1982, table 6.8). They also found that Catholic high schools were less racially segregated than public and that student achievement in Catholic schools was less related to socioeconomic background than was achievement in public schools.

Like the results of Coleman's 1966 study, these were challenged. Almost immediately, a series of studies appeared questioning the methods used (e.g., Alexander and Pallas, 1982; Goldberger and Cain, 1982; Noell, 1982). There were also supportive studies. Andrew Greeley, using the same HS&B database, found that minority students not only did better academically in Catholic high schools than in public schools, but the difference was largest for those youth with the poorest, lowest-educated parents (Greeley, 1982).

But the more important critiques came a year later when the sophomore follow-up data became available (e.g., Alexander and

Pallas, 1983; Willms, 1984). Coleman and Hoffer used the new HS&B data to do a value-added estimate and showed that lower–socioeconomic background 1980 sophomores made significantly larger test score gains in Catholic schools than in public schools, essentially the same results that they had found with the earlier data, but now using value-added analysis (Coleman and Hoffer, 1987). The other studies made two critiques. First, Coleman and coauthors had overestimated the Catholic school effect. Second, the gains on the tests from sophomore to senior year were, in any case, very small. Because the gains are so small overall, expressing them in year equivalents, as was done in the two Coleman studies, tends to make it seem that Catholic schools have a large advantage, when in fact the average test score difference between sophomore and senior year in public and Catholic schools combined is less than 0.3 standard deviation. So a 1-year gain is 0.15 standard deviation, and two-thirds of that is 0.1 standard deviation. Is this a large effect size? Most analysts agree that it is very small. Alexander and Pallas (1987) put it this way: "Jencks (1985) perceived these implications of our analyses and suggested two possibilities: Either the HS&B tests are not sufficiently sensitive to what is taught in school, or there is not much cognitive growth altogether in the last two years of high school" (pp. 107–108).

Willms (1987) argues further that blacks and Hispanics attending Catholic schools had similarly small achievement gains compared to similar students in public schools. Willms and others measure gains in terms of standard deviations from the mean and *effect sizes* (relative test score gains measured in standard deviations of test scores). A standard deviation of test score shows the test score difference between students who score at the mean (50th percentile) and those who score either at the 16th percentile at the low end or the 84th percentile at the high end. The effect size is a test score gain expressed in terms of standard deviations. It is a useful measure because it lets us compare gains by different groups of students on the same test or compare gains on different tests. A gain of 1 standard deviation is very large. It means that students increased their test scores from the 50th to the 84th percentile. So an effect size of 0.3 standard deviation resulting from a particular policy or from attending one type of school versus another would be meaningful. On the five main tests in the HS&B data, the Catholic school effect ranges from 0.11 to 0.16 standard deviation for blacks and 0.11 to 0.21 for Hispanics. "This modest effect is roughly equivalent to changing a student's performance in the class from the fiftieth to the fifty-fourth percentile" (Willms, 1987, p. 127).

Anthony Bryk and his former students, Valerie Lee and Peter Holland, also took the same HS&B data, used a somewhat different statistical analysis, and, like Coleman and Hoffer (1987), found a statistically significant Catholic school effect, again mainly for low-income African-American students (Bryk, Lee, and Holland, 1993). Their study tried to explain why Catholic education might be more successful with low-income pupils and what public schools could learn from this experience. We will come back to their argument momentarily.

Before doing so, let's return to Coleman. Whatever the size of the achievement effect of private as compared to public high school, Coleman became convinced that publicly funded private education as a possible alternative to public schooling had come of age—that the role of private education was distinctly different than it had been in the past. In a short preface to a two-volume symposium on choice and control in American education (Clune and Witte, 1990), Coleman (1990) argued that

> while a single common school made sense in the context of 1890 [a largely rural society], it does not make sense in 1990. The more appropriate answer, both within the public sector, and a system of education including private schools, is to expand parental choice and control at the school level. This will lead to increasing diversity and innovation in education, and will enhance community, an element that we seem to have lost in our current public education system. (p. ix)

We are not going to get into the issue of choice and its relevance to American society 100 years ago and today. One could question Coleman's characterization of Americans in the 1890s as being inward looking, very diverse, and information poor and, in the 1990s, as being much more culturally homogeneous and information rich. We also have doubts about his claim that the state (government) is no longer needed as an integrative agent or as an agent of socialization into a common set of moral values—that families choosing among a diversity of privately offered alternatives will end up doing better than in the public sector. All of this may or may not be the case. The vast majority of American parents still believe that public schools are where they want their children to be. They may want more choice, but recent votes in California and Michigan overwhelmingly rejecting voucher plans suggest that they do not want their tax dollars used to support private school alternatives. Polling data show that the proportion of Americans in favor of school vouchers for private schooling started at 24 percent in 1993, rose to 44 percent in 1997, and dropped to 34 percent by 2001. Public opposition to contracting private companies to run the public school system is also growing. The percentage of American parents opposing this practice rose from 59 percent in 1996 to 72 percent (Rose and Gallup, 2001). In short, Coleman's view does not appear to be widely held. The groups with the greatest doubts about public education are lowincome parents who have consistently perceived themselves are being shortchanged on school quality (Bositis, 1999). But as these groups searching for diversity in educational environments or rather for greater opportunity to learn the skills needed for economic success?

Coleman makes yet another argument, this one supporting private religious schools as just as valid a contender for the title of "common school" as the traditional neighborhood public version.

He contends that traditional concepts of local community, based on notions of shared workplaces and shared ethnicity, tied together by physical residential proximity (neighborhood), are quickly disappearing. Furthermore, residence is now highly segregated by class and race. This means, he claims, that the common school as defined by the public sector is no longer common. "In this kind of society, parental choice of school cannot destroy the common school; it has already been destroyed by residential stratification" (Coleman, 1990, p. xix). Thus, according to Coleman's construction of urban history, parental choice can no longer destroy community because the traditional notion of community no longer exists. To the contrary, by allowing parents to choose schools for their children on the basis of communities to which they do belong, that is, choosing religiously based schools, for instance, choice can strengthen some notion of community.

Coleman is correct that residential segregation in America's northern urban centers was likely to be based on ethnicity in the 1890s rather than on race or class, but class and racial stratification took place not long afterward with industrialization and black migration from the South (Zunz, 1982). Furthermore, cities such as New York, which had industrialized earlier, were already class segregated by the turn of the century (Ravitch, 1974). That said, why would Coleman consider a school attended largely by German-American or Polish-American children in Detroit or Chicago in 1900 a "common school"? True, families had a sense that it was a community school, and it may have cut across social classes within a particular ethnic group, but it was not "common" in the sense that it brought mainly low income Polish-origin children in contact with mainly middle income English-origin children.[2] These groups tended to live in different parts of town even in 1900 (Zunz, 1982). Coleman's main concern is that the neighborhood school serving African-American or Puerto Rican children in a place such as New York in 2000 is a segregated, poor school, but this was just as true for blacks in Detroit or Chicago or Birmingham in 1920 as in 2000, perhaps even more so.

As an alternative to building community through choice, couldn't the current urban neighborhood fulfill this role? Coleman's argument about the decline of community may indeed be correct, but he is off the mark in terms of public schools' role in building community. The Deweyan ideal of the "school as social centre" is still current (Dewey, 1976). Public schools are still widely recognized as focal points for community revitalization and integration, where schools not only strive to serve children's academic needs, but also play a vital role in providing necessary social support services, linking families to their broader environment and fostering social and institutional networks (Harkavy, 1998). Several of our case studies attest to this fact. Indeed, the local public school may well be refashioned as a community center in an economy and society built on knowledge and information (Carnoy, 2000).

The two parts of Coleman's argument in which we are particularly interested are his claim that public education is to blame for lack of parent participation (Coleman, 1990, p. xiv) and his claim that private schools expand the variety of choice available to parents and hence increase the probability that parents will participate in their children's education (Coleman, 1990, p. xviii). If Coleman is correct, parents with children now in private schools should be more involved in their children's schooling than parents of similar socioeconomic background with children in public schools.

Bryk, Lee, and and Holland (1993) turned Coleman's case for private religious education on its head. Rather than supporting Coleman's case that parents' choice of religious-based education can strengthen community, they argue that Catholic education is organized around a set of communitarian values that help disconnected low-income urban students to do better academically. Their argument places the locus of community values in the organization of the school, not the religious affiliation of the parents. For Bryk, Lee, and Holland, the focus is not on building a larger community, but on improving student academic performance. They do not quite make the case that Catholic education should expand at the expense of public. Instead, they argue that public schools can incorporate the organizational lessons of Catholic education that make it so much more successful for low-income students. These lessons are to make public high schools smaller, more intimate places with a real sense of community and purpose and to focus as much as possible on a college preparatory academic curriculum for all students, rather than the severe tracking that occurs in public schools.

These arguments are logical and interesting, but Bryk, Lee, and Holland face the same issues as Coleman in maintaining that Catholic high schools add much more achievement even for low-income minority students than do public schools. Mathematics scores for lower-income students are significantly higher in Catholic schools in both sophomore and senior years. But the difference in raw scores for minority students only increases by about 1.4 points on a 38-item test over the 2 years (Bryk, Lee, and Holland, 1993, figure 10.2). Should we privatize the schools or overhaul the public schools to get 1.4 more points on a 38-point math test?

A somewhat more convincing case for Catholic high schools is made by Evans and Schwab (1995) and Neal (1997), who argue that students in Catholic high schools are much more likely to complete with their cohort than similar students in public high schools and are much more likely to attend college.[3] These results suggest that Catholic high schools place more emphasis on academic, college-bound courses and do more to get their students into college, as argued by Coleman, Hoffer, and Kilgore and Bryk, Lee, and Holland. However, it is difficult to tell whether Catholic high schools find it easier to do this than public schools because they are more academic and, through their strong sense of community and discipline, can encourage lower–socioeconomic background students to try harder, therefore enabling them to gain the credits that they need to go on to college, or whether they can attract a more selective clientele as well as be more selective of their student body and, hence, can better emphasize academics.

William Sander (2001) tries to capture this possible selectivity by correcting attainment data for religiosity (church attendance), whether students are Catholic or not. He deems that this correction is important, because religiosity has been shown to have a positive effect on academic achievement. Hence, without excluding religiosity from statistical studies on achievement, the effect of Catholic schools might be confounded with religiosity. Sander finds that this correction eliminates the difference in high school graduation rate for all but inner-city minority youth, who, given similar social background and religious affiliation as comparable students, do have a much higher probability of graduating from Catholic than from public high schools. He summarizes his findings in the following manner:

> Although Catholic schools are probably not better than public schools on the average, some Catholic schools are probably superior to the public schools in a community. This is probably the case for blacks and Hispanics in big cities. Catholic schools in inner-city areas that disproportionately serve a low-income population are probably more efficient than public schools, at least at the high-school level. (Sander, 2001, p. 22)

So far, we have only discussed the results for students in high school. The data are much scarcer for private (Catholic) versus public primary and middle schools, the focus of our study in this book. Sander (1996) finds a positive achievement effect for students attending Catholic primary schools, but this effect disappears when non-Catholics (10 percent of students attending Catholic schools) are removed from the sample. A more recent study by Jepsen (2000) finds no Catholic school effect in primary school on mathematics scores, but a positive effect on reading scores. So even though advocates of privatization rely heavily on claims of higher achievement of low-income, minority pupils in Catholic schools to make their case for vouchers and charter schools, the evidence backing these claims is at best ambiguous and inconclusive.

THE NEW EMPIRICISM AND THE CASE FOR EDUCATIONAL MARKETS

At about the same time that Bryk, Lee, and Holland were publishing journal articles that formed the basis for their broad study of Catholic education and a number of analysts were showing that the differences in achievement gains between Catholic and public high schools were minimal, another study was being written using the same High School and Beyond survey. This study, by two political scientists, John Chubb and Terry Moe, came to a quite different conclusion than either Coleman, Hoffer, and Kilgore or Bryk, Lee, and Holland (Chubb and Moe, 1990). Chubb and Moe concluded that students in private high schools (mainly Catholic schools) made larger test score gains in tenth to twelfth grade than students in public high schools because private schools competed in a marketplace, whereas public schools did not.

Chubb and Moe began working together in the early 1980s, when both were assistant professors of political science at Stanford. Both were interested in bureaucracy, and Chubb was especially interested in federal funding of education. When Coleman's research comparing public and Catholic education appeared in 1982, Chubb and Moe became interested in the High School and Beyond data. The National Center for Educational Statistics was about to resurvey the high schools in the original sample, this time asking further questions about school organization. Chubb and Moe were able to put in some questions. The data in this survey, called the *Administrator and Teacher Supplement* (ATS) to the HS&B, became and important part of their empirical analysis.

"We saw Coleman's analysis and thought we could do something more sophisticated," Moe told us, "getting more data on organization and performance of schools. We wanted to know what it was about the schools that was better, not just that students scored higher. We were data oriented, and wanted to do a better job of explaining differences."

At the same time, both were developing political theories of the way that organizations behaved and, ultimately, these were the ideas that drove how they interpreted their empirical results. Their conception of bureaucracies, including public school bureaucracies, as evolving out of democracy and competing interest groups and forcing institutions such as schools to become stratified and ossified, emerged from the discussions that the two had during the mid-1980s. They were together at The Brookings Institution in 1984 to 1986, but Moe returned to Stanford while Chubb stayed on in Washington. Finally, in the late 1980s, they combined the empirical results with their political theory to write *Politics, Markets, and America's Schools* (Chubb and Moe, 1990).

Their purpose, Moe told us, was to do "a good social science book." But the moment was also propitious to create a splash with a policy formulation that made waves. Brookings also thought the book might have a big impact. Eight years of the Reagan administration had just ended, with a lot more discussion of choice, vouchers, and privatization. Milwaukee's voucher experiment was just starting and the social choice movement was at a pivotal stage.

So rather than simply focus on the empirical results and what they might show about their theories of bureaucracy and democracy, Chubb and Moe embraced choice and vouchers as the logical policy outcome of their study. This was not a big leap. They had come to believe that the public educational system was trapped in a bureaucratic logic that would not allow it to produce the kind of teaching and learning possible in a competitive, privately managed system.

Chubb and Moe's argument is made on two levels. The first is that effective and ineffective schools differ in their organizational characteristics. Good high schools (those that produce relatively high increases in test scores between tenth and twelfth grade) have clearer goals, better leadership, more emphasis on academic coursework, and a higher level of teacher collegiality, influence, and status. The second level is that these organizational differences are not random; rather, they are the result of different *political environments.* These political environments are the cause of organizational differences in schools and hence differences in school effectiveness. Chubb and Moe argue that the key predictor of effective school organization is school autonomy, and school autonomy is, in turn, a function of whether a school is private, subject to market forces of competition and choice, or public, that is, bureaucratically controlled. They conclude that only through transforming America's educational system from democratic control to market-driven can schools be significantly improved.

Their theory is that "the politics of democratic control promotes the piece-by-piece construction of a peculiar set of organizational arrangements that are highly bureaucratic" (p. 44) and that the "institutions of democratic control [in public education] are inherently destructive of school autonomy and inherently conducive to bureaucracy" (p. 47). From this, they argue that

> America's public schools are governed by institutions of direct democratic control, and their organizations should be expected to bear the indelible stamp of those institutions. They should tend to be highly bureaucratic and systematically lacking in the requisites of effective performance. Private schools, on the other hand, operate in a very different institutional setting distinguished by the basic features of markets—decentralization, competition, and choice—and their organizations should be expected to bear a very different stamp as a result. They should tend to possess the autonomy, clarity of mission, strong leadership, teacher professionalism, and team cooperation that public schools want but (except under very fortunate circumstances) are unlikely to have. (p. 67)

Chubb and Moe go on to describe differences between public and private schools in terms of personnel, school goals, leadership, and educational practice. On all counts, public schools end up serving bureaucratic needs rather than educational ones, whereas private schools, autonomous and subject to the demands of choice and competition, must necessarily focus on educational goals and getting the job done. Private schools are also much freer to do what they want—principals can fire bad teachers, hire teachers that are in tune with the school's goals, and teachers have more time to teach, rather than filling out paperwork.

> First, they [teachers] are required to follow the rules that cause them to depart from what they might otherwise do, and thus to behave in ways that contradict or fail to take advantage of their professional expertise and judgment. Second, they are required to spend time and effort documenting, usually through formal paperwork, that they have in fact followed these rules . . . (p. 59). In a market setting, principals and teachers are likely to have a great deal of discretion in determining school practices . . . Schools can be clear, bold, and controversial in the practices they adopt as long as they attract a specialized clientele that values what they do. . . . (p. 60)

This characterization of schools as divided along a public–private axis is the key to Chubb and Moe's analysis. Their theory argues that this is the way that public and private schools should differ, and their empirical work, using the High School and Beyond data, is geared to show that these are, indeed, the way that private and public schools really *do* differ.

However interesting and sweeping their attempt to make the case for markets in education, close scrutiny of their work raises serious questions. From our standpoint, the main issue is whether the characterization of public and private education predicted by Chubb and Moe's theory is borne out by empirical evidence.

John Witte (1992) and Anthony Bryk and Valerie Lee (1992) argue persuasively that it is not. Witte makes a strong case that

Chubb and Moe's analysis of the data is slanted to make the difference in student performance between high- and low-scoring schools much larger than it actually is. He also shows that Chubb and Moe make major policy claims based on estimated equations that only explain a very small fraction of the variation in student achievement scores. This is analogous to claiming that we know which children will make gains on their test scores, but only predict correctly on one out of twenty.

Bryk and Lee (1992) argue that Chubb and Moe choose to overlook an obvious outcome of their own data analysis: the "bureaucratic problem" of public schools—even the way that they define it—is concentrated in large *urban* public schools, rather than in public schools as a whole. Their evidence shows that urban location is the most important variable in explaining the level of administrative and personnel constraints (bureaucratic controls), followed by private control (table 5.12). Chubb and Moe's calculations do not take into consideration that the likelihood of a public school student being in an urban environment is appreciably greater than the likelihood of a private school student being in an urban environment. Thus, if the combined effect on student achievement of being in an urban and public school (compared, for example, to being in a suburban private school) were teased out, Bryk and Lee argue that the "urban" effect would be more salient than the "public" effect. "If this proved to be the case," Bryk and Lee contend, "it would appear then that bureaucratic constraints and ineffective school organization are principally an *urban public school* problem and not a more general democratic governance problem. Suddenly, the Chubb and Moe results begin to look more like an argument for radical decentralization of urban public school in order to jolt bureaucratic calcification and revive democratic control!" (Bryk and Lee, 1992, p. 447).

The contrast between Bryk, Lee, and Holland's (1993) and Chubb and Moe's (1990) interpretation of the same data hinges on the following issue. Since much of the Bryk, Lee, and Holland results had appeared in journal articles before 1990, their approach was not just a reaction to Chubb and Moe. From the start, the two groups of analysts had different views of what they were trying to show about the educational system. They both took their cue from Coleman, Hoffer, and Kilgore's (1982) earlier work. They both ended up agreeing that school autonomy is an important cause of better student performance in private schools. They also ended up agreeing that schools' approach to academic work makes a difference. But Chubb and Moe chose to ignore the particularities of their school sample and the particularities of which groups in which location are most affected by these differences and so end up interpreting their findings as a private school effect, hence a market effect. In their interpretation, public schools have little autonomy and, under bureaucratic dicta, end up tracking students, thus lowering academic performance.

Bryk, Lee, and Holland focus on Catholic versus public school differences and how they affect *particular* groups, that is, lower-income versus higher-income students. Since the differences in performance between Catholic and public schools are concentrated in lower-income students, it seems logical that whatever Catholic schools are doing differently has implications mainly for lower, not higher, socioeconomic background students. Family income of students attending Catholic high schools in the early 1980s was much higher, on average, than for public high school students (Coleman, Hoffer, and Kilgore, 1982, table 3-5). So low-income students, including the relatively small percentage of black students that attended Catholic high schools in 1980,[4] were (and continue to be) more likely to be in schools with higher-income students than if they attended their local public high school. Furthermore, in the early 1980s, a high percentage of black and Hispanic students attending Catholic schools came from relatively high income families (Catterall, 1988, table 7). Public high schools are likely to be more homogeneous (and segregated) because of the residential definition of their student bodies.

Far from interpreting this as a market effect, Bryk, Lee, and Holland suggest that there is something special about Catholic schools that is rooted in their historical mission in Protestant America. This mission developed a school with a particular sense of community, and it is this community that today allows them to integrate low-income students into more demanding academic courses. It is true that because of white urban flight in the 1960s Catholic schools began accepting considerable numbers of minority non-Catholics in the 1970s. Even so, as discussed above, Catholic schools have a smaller percentage of minority students than public schools even in urban areas, and the education of the parents of these minority students is, on average, higher than the education of parents of minority students in public schools. Furthermore, Catholic high schools have tended to become more middle class, not less, in the 20 years since the HS&B data were collected, although the meaning of this trend has been bitterly debated (see Baker and Riordan, 1999a, 1999b; Greeley, 1999a, 1999b). Baker and Riordan argue that by becoming more elite, even as their student body becomes less Catholic and has higher minority representation (increasingly Hispanic, for example), Catholic secondary schools are becoming less of a model alternative for inner-city urban public schools.

Over time, it also became increasingly difficult to staff Catholic schools with religious personnel. As a result, the Church changed some aspects of Catholic education, making it less traditional and more open. This could be interpreted as a market response—the need to compete with public schools and other private schools for students. But Bryk, Lee, and Holland make a persuasive case that higher academic performance among low-income students is not a product of changes designed to attract this new clientele. Rather, they claim that the historic mission deeply imbedded in the American version of Catholic education is especially well suited to the academic and social needs of low-income urban students. Furthermore, many of the aspects of Catholic education—community, a focus on academic course work, smaller school size, required parent commitment—could be incorporated into public schools. These identifiable school characteristics, then, are not primarily determined by the need to compete for students, but rather by the traditions of an educational system developed in the nineteenth and early twentieth centuries.[5]

Chubb and Moe's estimated relationship of organizational differences to differences in achievement seems to be the result of highly situational context. More school autonomy (i.e., private control) in urban areas has a positive impact primarily on lower-income students. If the market were the main explanation for such positive achievement effects, certainly private schools would have an achievement advantage over suburban, "shopping mall," public high schools. Yet that does not seem to be the case. The democratic imperative and resulting educational bureaucracy may result in less than optimal conditions in these suburban public schools, but private high schools do not seem to do significantly better, autonomy or no.

Put another way, Murnane (1984) has argued that "even the largest estimates of private school advantage are small relative to the variation in quality among different public schools, among different Catholic schools, and among different non-Catholic private schools. Consequently, in predicting the quality of a student's education, it is less important to know whether the student attended a public school or a private school, than it is to know which school within a particular sector the student attended" (p. 207).

This raises the issue of how selective urban Catholic schools are when it comes to these lower-income students and the role that student selection plays in explaining differences in student achievement between private and public schools. In the early 1980s, only about 2 percent of low-income black families, about 4 percent of Hispanic families, and 5 percent of low-income white families sent their children to private secondary schools (Catterall, 1988, table 7). In the early 1990s, Catholic high schools had a higher fraction of their student body that were black or Hispanic, but the average socioeconomic class of these students was higher than that of students who attended public school and was apparently rising relative to the public school population (Baker and Riordan, 1999a). Furthermore, it is important to ask how representative of students coming from minority low-income groups were and are these private school students?

All the studies using the HS&B data take into account socioeconomic background differences among students in the sample when estimating the private or Catholic school effect. Both Chubb and Moe and Bryk, Lee, and Holland also control for sophomore test score when estimating senior test score. They base their interpretation of differential achievement largely on gain scores. Socioeconomic background and a baseline test score are *observable* student differences that could explain greater or smaller achievement gains regardless of what schools do. But private schools know much more about their students than is measured by their parents' education, income, and so forth—the items that appear in the data set. The schools know their parents' commitment to their children's education, the students' social behavior, and the students' work habits. These *nonobservable* (from the standpoint of survey data collection) differences could bias the results. If parents *self-select* on motivation, commitment to their child's academic success, and other unobservables, the social background data will not produce unbiased estimates of what the achievement gains would be if more typical students were to enroll in private schools. If private schools are good at selecting their students from among a group that might on average perform poorly in school, they may just be "cream-skimming," rather than actually producing a more positive academic result by something that they do in the classroom. If researchers are unable to identify such unobserved student attributes, they tend to overestimate greater achievement gains produced by the school.[6]

VOUCHER EXPERIMENTS AND VOUCHER INITIATIVES

The first voucher experiment was in the Alum Rock school district in San Jose, California, in the early 1970s. It was undertaken as one of a series of educational experiments initiated by the Nixon administration. In Alum Rock, parents were allowed to choose among a number of "minischool" alternative programs organized within public schools (Elmore, 1993, p. 301). The number of programs increased from twenty-two to fifty-one during the 4 years of the experiment. Parents were allowed to choose among programs in any voucher schools, and those children who chose to participate were provided transportation if it meant attending a nonneighborhood school.

Because the vouchers were restricted to programs within public schools, they tell us about choice behavior among parents, not private–public differences. Even so, the results are instructive and are borne out by choice research in later voucher programs and research on charter school choice. Surveys done in Alum Rock showed that voucher parents were more knowledgeable about program options than those who did not participate. Participating parents' knowledge was positively related to their expectations and aspirations for their children, and this, in turn, was positively related to parents' education and income. Geographical location of the alternative programs was the single most important factor entering into parent choice, but this seemed to decline over time as parents became more aware of the choices available. The proportion of children in Alum Rock attending nonneighborhood schools increased from 11 to 22 percent in 4 years (Elmore, 1993, p. 307).

The main reason for the Alum Rock experiment was to test whether choice produced distinctly different educational options for students and, as a result, higher achievement for students whose parents put them into voucher programs. Neither seemed to have occurred. Classroom observations revealed no significant differences among voucher classes or between voucher and nonvoucher classes. Reading scores were not significantly different among voucher classes and not significantly higher in voucher classrooms than in nonvoucher classrooms (Elmore, 1993, p. 311). By the end of the Alum Rock demonstration project, the only real effect seemed to be that parents had gotten a choice and about one-fifth of the parents had taken advantage of it. Many parents supported choice and liked it, but most were not willing to transport their children to other schools.

The next voucher experiment was not conducted until the early 1990s, almost 20 years later and in a very different political environment. The experiment in Milwaukee was initiated by the state legislature and specifically focused on private schools as an alternative to public schools. The Milwaukee experiment was followed by many others, some initiated by states, but most by private donors. At the same time, states such as Minnesota put in place public school choice programs. Other states, Arizona, California, and Michigan foremost, initiated legislation that promoted charter schools. These are autonomous schools organized mainly within the framework of public education. But some states allow private schools to reorganize as charters and receive full public funding. Finally, electors in two states got to vote on statewide voucher initiatives, two in California (1993 and 2000) and one in Michigan (2000). Both failed, but voucher advocates could certainly claim that this was the beginning of a national swing toward a new political consciousness shift in education.

Voucher politics in the 1990s became increasingly complex. The movement encompassed two distinct driving forces, one, a conservative, free-market ideology that prefers private to public provision of any services, and the second, the practical demands of low-income parents for better schooling, public or private. Even if private schools were no more effective than public schools, free-market reformers would insist that vouchers make parents and children better off because of choice and competition and that private school choice should be made available to all parents, regardless of income. But the demand in inner cities for better schooling was based not on free-market ideology, but on academic results.

Whatever the origin of their support for vouchers, advocates have felt the need to support two claims empirically. The first claim is that private schools financed by public funds can do a better job than public schools of educating the children most at risk of school failure, whether because vouchers are a route to smaller classes and better teachers or because private schools are superior in other respects. The second claim is that vouchers increase incentives for public schools to improve by threatening low-performing public schools with the loss of students to competing private schools.

The voucher experiment in Milwaukee began in 1991 on the initiative of Polly Williams, an African-American Wisconsin legislator. The $2,500 vouchers were awarded by lottery to low-income families, 75 percent African Americans, to be used only in secular private schools. Schools had to accept the voucher as full payment (parents could not top it up). Initially, seven private schools agreed to take voucher students. Although the legislature set a maximum of 1,500 vouchers to be awarded, this number was never attained during the 5 years of the program. Enrollment increased steadily but slowly, from 341 in school year 1990–1991 to 830 in 1994–1995. The number of schools participating also increased, from seven in 1990–1991 and six in 1991–1992 to 11 in 1992–1993 and 12 in 1994–1995 and 1995–1996. Later, in 1997, when the Wisconsin legislature expanded the program to include religious schools, enrollment in voucher schools increased substantially. In the school year 2001–2002, about ten thousand Milwaukee children attended private schools using vouchers.

The legislature commissioned University of Wisconsin professor John Witte and his colleagues to study the students who received vouchers and compare their achievement with similar students in public schools. Witte and coauthors found high levels of satisfaction among families receiving vouchers (Witte, Sterr, and Thorn, 1995). Yet, when they analyzed achievement differences between those Milwaukee pupils who used vouchers to attend "choice schools" and Milwaukee public school pupils of similar socioeconomic background, race, and ethnicity, they found that, generally, voucher students did no better in either math or reading. The one exception was a statistically significant *negative* effect of attending choice schools on reading scores in the second school year of the program (1991–1992). According to Witte and coauthors, many of the poorest choice students left the program at the end of that second year. The authors also estimated the achievement effect controlling for the number of years that the choice students had been in a private school. Again, private school voucher students did no better than public school students in either math or reading. The only effect that approached statistical significance was a negative reading score for those who had been in private schools for 2 years.

Witte, Sterr, and Thorn (1995) admitted that such an analysis has its limits, since many new students were being added to the private school sample every year, and a large fraction (about 30 percent) left the sample. The proportion leaving the sample was about the same for public school pupils. So the sample of private and public school pupils differed from year to year.

Other factors also changed in Milwaukee from year to year. The initial voucher was about one-half of Milwaukee's public school per-pupil spending. The voucher rose quickly, with private schools demanding and getting a higher voucher, until it was close to the primary school public cost per pupil when special-education costs are accounted for. This is a major reason that more private schools were attracted into the program and more students could be accommodated in later years. Even so, over the course of the experiment, several of the participating private schools closed, including some due to bankruptcy.

Witte's results were challenged by others, namely Harvard political scientist Paul Peterson and his colleagues, who argued that Witte's methodology biased the private gains downward and that students in private schools had, in fact, made large gains over the 4 years, particularly in mathematics (Greene, Peterson, and Du, 1996). These results were then challenged by Witte (Witte, 1997) and, in a separate analysis, by Princeton public policy analyst Cecilia Rouse. Her results estimated a relatively small relative gain in math scores for voucher students in the third and fourth years (Rouse, 1998a). She also estimated that students in a public magnet school program with smaller class sizes had much larger gains (Rouse, 1998b).

In 1997 the Wisconsin legislature expanded the voucher program to a maximum of 15,000 low-income students and included religious schools. The legislation was upheld by the Wisconsin Supreme Court. Initially, about 8,000 students took up the vouchers, which continued to be worth about the cost of Milwaukee's per-pupil spending on primary education ($5,500 in 1997). In the first year, about one-third of voucher takers under this expanded program were already in private schools, but qualified because of their low family incomes. By the school year 2001–2002, about 10,000 children used vouchers at over 100 mostly religious private schools (Williams, 2000).[7] This is a significant fraction of Milwaukee's 100,000 public school students. Even if only 7,500 of the voucher students transferred from public schools, the voucher program has shifted almost 8 percent of Milwaukee's public school students to private schools. This suggests that, given a large enough voucher, a significant number of low-income families will take advantage of it, and at least some new schools will come into the market. However, no one knows whether voucher students are performing better in this expanded program because, unlike public school students, they are not required by the legislature to take state tests, and no evaluation program is written into the legislation. We also know little about how many students who took up vouchers returned to public schools after a year or two in a private school. Over one quarter of students receiving vouchers for the past three years opted not to renew them (Public Policy Forum, 2002)

Cleveland's voucher program was approved by the Ohio legislature in June 1995 and began in the 1996–1997 school year with a maximum voucher of $2,500. Voucher recipients were chosen by lottery and received a fixed percentage of tuition charged by private schools, the percentage depending on the family's income level. Students whose family income was at or above 200 percent of the poverty line received 75 percent of the school's tuition up to $2,500, and those below the poverty line received 90 percent, up to $2,500.

The Cleveland program differed from the Milwaukee experiment in several important aspects. In Cleveland, more than twice as many vouchers were offered as in Milwaukee (3,700 versus 1,500). Unlike Milwaukee families, Cleveland families had to add to the voucher to attend private schools, both because the voucher covered only part of tuition and because private schools could charge tuition higher than the voucher. As in Milwaukee, the program got off to a slow start, with only about 1,500 students taking advantage of the vouchers.[8] A fraction (about 25 percent) of Cleveland's vouchers were offered to families with children already in private schools, and vouchers in Cleveland could be used in religious schools, as they later could in the expanded Milwaukee program. About 80 percent of families in the Cleveland program sent their children to Catholic and other parochial schools.

Nearly all the others went to Hope Schools, two private for-profit schools created by David Brennan, a wealthy entrepreneur and major contributor to Ohio's Republican Party, especially to take advantage of voucher availability. Brennan had been instrumental in getting the voucher program through the Ohio legislature. But once the Hope schools went into operation, he realized that his schools were losing money at the $2,500 voucher level. He tried unsuccessfully to get the legislature to raise the value of the voucher. Because Ohio also provides for charter schools, funding them at about the same amount per student as public schools, Brennan converted the Hope Schools into charters to take advantage of the higher levels of financing. This left almost all voucher students attending religious schools. On December 11, 2000, the 6th Circuit Federal Court of Appeals upheld a lower-court ruling that these vouchers gave unconstitutional aid to religious schools. The U.S. Supreme Court, however, overturned this ruling on June 27, 2002 paving the way for the continuation of this scheme, as well as its potential expansion throughout the country. In the 2001–2002 school year, 4,456 Cleveland students in kindergarten through eighth grade opted for a voucher to attend primarily private religious schools.

Evaluations of Cleveland vouchers are in even greater disagreement than the Milwaukee analyses. The bottom line is that gains for voucher students in religious schools may have been somewhat positive in language arts and science, but not other subjects. Gains in the for-profit Hope Schools appear to have been negative (Metcalf, 2001).

By the late 1990s, a series of small, privately financed voucher experiments had been started in a number of cities, aimed at low-income blacks and Hispanics. The amount of the voucher in the cities (New York City; Dayton, Ohio; Washington, D.C.; and Charlotte, North Carolina) range from $1,500 to $1,700. The main purpose of these experiments was to show that vouchers had a positive effect on low-income student achievement and to drum up support for vouchers nationwide.

The results from these smaller voucher experiments show similar satisfaction gains as in Milwaukee and Cleveland, but much larger achievement gains from using a voucher in private schools, at least for African-American students (Howell et al., 2000; Mayer et al., 2002). The authors of the second-year round of studies claim that their results are better than those done in Milwaukee and Cleveland because of the truly experimental design of the evaluation. Students in these new experiments are assigned vouchers at random from a pool of low-income applicants, and both voucher recipients who go on to private schools and nonrecipients who stay in public school are tested annually to measure achievement gains. Researchers claim that such random assignment allows for unbiased comparisons between gains made by low-income students attending private and public schools.

However, this strategy does not speak to other issues. The new studies suffer from serious potential biases. One is that families who did not receive a voucher may have suffered *disappointment effects* that would lower their children's performance in public school below the level that they might have achieved had they never applied for the voucher. Another possible source of bias is that these voucher experiments are marked by consistently low participation rates in follow-up tests. Only in New York did more than one-half the students take the first- and second-year follow-up tests.[9] In Washington, D.C., the decline in participation between the first- and second-year follow-up is particularly large: about 25 percent of the sample dropped out from the testing after the first year. The researchers are unable to correct for the possibility that those who did not come back to take the follow-up tests would have altered significantly the private–public school comparisons. A third source of possible bias is the concentration of gains in particular small cohorts in the sample. For example, the only New York City group of voucher recipients that showed statistically significant gains in achievement over their public school counterparts by the second year was the African-American voucher cohort entering fifth grade in the first year of the experiment. In the third-year follow-up study in New York, this group continued to make gains, and those who had begun in the third grade and stayed in private schools for 3 years also made significant gains in mathematics (Mayer et al., 2002). But the other cohorts did not experience a similar degree of progress. Yet the researchers concluded that African-American voucher recipients *as a whole* had made significant gains in New York. In Dayton, gains also varied enormously among cohorts in different grades (Carnoy, 2001).

Neither were Howell et al. (2000) able to explain why in New York City, with the largest of these small voucher experiments and a large group of Latino students in the sample, African-American students realized a positive effect on test scores from attending a private school, whereas Latino students did not. Private school characteristics as reported by parents, including class size, did not explain test score differences.[10] If peer effects play an important role in explaining whether students using vouchers make significant gains over their public school counterparts, we can assume that a voucher plan is likely to benefit relatively few low-income students, that is, mainly those who can get into existing (mainly Catholic) schools with already better performing students. If this is the case, vouchers are not likely to solve the problem of educating low-income students.

To muddle this picture even further, the year 3 data introduce even more questions with regard to private school effectiveness with African-American students. Although black students attending private schools in New York City showed consistent improvements on test scores vis-à-vis their public school counterparts, this effect has not held true for black children in the District of Columbia. In Washington, African-American students in private schools held an advantage over public school children after 2 years in the voucher program. Yet this advantage vanished by the third year (Viadero, 2002).

Another recent round of alternative studies argues that threats of vouchers or competition from voucher-induced private alternatives, including charter schools, significantly increase low-income student performance in affected private schools (Greene, 2001; Hoxby, 2001). In the late 1990s as well, the state of Florida implemented a voucher program as part of its statewide public school evaluation program. If a Florida public school performed poorly on state tests for 2 of 4 years, all students in that school would be offered a voucher to attend other schools, either private or public, of their choice. Jay Greene of the Manhattan Institute evaluated this program, indicating large effects on low-performing schools due to the voucher threat (Greene, 2001). He tried to make the case that the threat of vouchers in Florida for students in "failing" public schools caused math and writing gains among Florida's lowest-performing schools to increase significantly more than the gains experienced by higher-performing schools. The finding was widely publicized as "proving" that vouchers were an effective policy tool for improving education. But other studies of relative gains made in an earlier year in Florida and by failing schools in Texas and North Carolina show that, even without a voucher threat, failing schools made relative gains as large or larger than in Florida in 1999–2000 when vouchers were introduced (Carnoy, 2001). So Greene's results tell us little about whether the threat of vouchers—as opposed to the stigma associated with being labeled a failing school—actually makes low-performing public schools do better.

The Hoxby (2001) analysis of test scores in three cases—Milwaukee's expanded voucher program competing with low-income public schools, public schools competing with charter schools in Michigan, and public schools competing with charter schools in Arizona—ends up with mixed results, too. Arizona public schools in districts with a larger number of charter schools do no better than public schools in other districts; public school students in the few Michigan districts with five or more charter schools do significantly better than similar students in less competitive districts; and public schools with Milwaukee's lowest-income students made larger gains since the expansion of private schooling under the new voucher plan. Here again, however, it is difficult to attribute student achievement gains to competition. Competition from voucher or charter schools may have been the cause of public school improvement in these districts. But other influences, such as increased attention to test scores in Wisconsin and Michigan or the peculiarities of the few Michigan districts with more than five charters, may be, as in the Florida case, just as reasonable an explanation for increased test scores in public schools as increased competition.[11]

PRIVATIZING PUBLIC SCHOOLS

Another phenomenon emerged in the 1990s: private for-profit companies were formed to manage publicly funded schools on the premise that they could do a better job than public bureaucracies. Two new institutions emerged simultaneously. One was the charter school, a school organized by parents, teachers, or another private entity to receive public funds, but operate independently of school district control. Charters vary from state to state, but the conception is the same: by breaking free of most regulations governing public schools, charter schools can in theory deliver their own vision of a good education. They provide an alternative educational choice for parents in the public school district (Nathan, 1996; Wells, 1999).

The second institution was for-profit educational management. These firms derive their profit from subcontracting with either public or quasi-public (read charter) schools to administer everything from hiring and firing teachers to developing curriculum to contracting for janitorial services and buying books. The largest of these companies is Edison. Media entrepreneur Chris Whittle began Edison as an enterprise that would develop a nationwide chain of schools. Edison schools would deliver better education than public schools for the same cost as the national average of public school spending per pupil, about $6,400 in 1993. The capital investment for the venture proved too large, so Whittle converted Edison into a management company that would apply the Edison model to low-performing public schools, preferably reorganized as charter schools. Charter status gave Edison more freedom over teacher contracts and other aspects of school organization.

The results for private management companies running schools have been mixed. In the early 1990s for instance, Hartford and Baltimore contracted with Educational Alternatives, Inc., to manage some of their lowest-performing schools. The schools did not perform significantly better, and the contracts were not renewed.

Edison Schools, Inc., is probably the highest-profile private management company of public schools. It is now managing 132 schools in twenty-two states, and in April 2002 it was assigned the management responsibility for twenty schools within the School District of Philadelphia. Governor Mark Schweiker had originally sought to delegate to Edison control over the public school system, but he later retreated in face of opposition from parents, educators, and labor leaders. The company has had some successes, but in many of its schools test scores do not rise more rapidly than competing publicly run schools. In a study commissioned by the American Federation of Teachers comparing forty Edison schools with public schools serving similar populations, Edison students' performance shows mixed results (American Federation of Teachers, 2000). Ironically, Edison management, which has consistently argued that private management is more effective than school district bureaucracy, now faces many of the same problems as does the administration in a large urban school district. Some of its schools suffer from mediocre principals, issues with teachers, and major principal and teacher turnover.

The privately managed (charter) school is an attractive alternative for parents (and school districts) desperate to improve academic performance in low-performing schools. Any alternative that can improve children's learning is better than the status quo. If the current administration cannot do the job, parents argue, get someone else to do it. It is hard to contest that logic. But do these private companies actually do a better job? The evidence is hardly clear.

WHERE ARE WE?

In many ways, this all leaves us back at square one. We can imagine that well-organized private schools could outperform public schools. But many public schools are also well organized. Should we really expect private schools to do better with students than public schools? Are private schools inherently more effective, meaning that they can produce better academic results with children of the same socioeconomic background than public schools?

The empirical results of many studies comparing achievement differences in voucher schools and privately managed schools with like students in public schools suggest that the differences are at best small. Furthermore, there is enormous variation among both private and public schools. Many private schools do worse than public schools; others do better. Obviously, being private does not guarantee higher quality. Being public does not necessarily mean lower quality.

More than generalized student achievement differences that result from significant differences between private (market driven) and public schools, the empirical studies may suggest something else. By allowing parents, particularly African-American, low-income parents, access to a limited number of places in existing private (Catholic) schools, some of their children will be more successful than in public schools. Thus, despite the claims that private education is better than public, the achievement comparisons among secondary school students from large surveys and among primary school students from voucher experiments do not provide convincing evidence that private schools do anything different to induce more learning than do public schools.

Nevertheless, we wanted to see for ourselves. So, to get behind these numbers and behind the ideological rhetoric of markets versus bureaucracy, we have designed a model to understand how a school works and applied this model in a number of private and public schools.

[2]

ARE PRIVATE
AND PUBLIC SCHOOLS
ORGANIZED DIFFERENTLY?

When we take stock of the empirical results, the notion that private schools are more effective than public schools is not as clear as voucher and choice advocates would have us believe. Students from similar family backgrounds appear to score only slightly higher on tests when they attend private schools, but this is only at the secondary level and has been reliably tested only for Catholic schools. Neither are the results likely to be completely free of selection bias, despite researchers' efforts to correct for differences among students attending public and private schools.

Although a majority of children attending private schools do so in elementary education, the data on private elementary schools is so sparse that we cannot say much at all about achievement differences at this level. And, although the reliable results only apply to pupils in Catholic secondary schools, nowadays almost half of private school pupils do not attend Catholic schools but go to a variety of mainly religious schools of other denominations. Researchers know little if anything about the academic performance of these students.

So we know that some students attending private schools perform better academically than those attending a public school. Still, based on the empirical results, our best guess would be that the vast majority of students make about the same academic gains whether they attend one type of school or the other.

Most Americans would probably find this surprising, especially after being bombarded for more than a decade by negative commentaries about public education. Yet, based on the cold facts of test score comparisons for like students, private schools at best do only slightly better than their public counterparts in raising achievement.

However, private schools could still be very different from public schools in other ways. Parents do not judge the goodness of schools only on academic grounds. They may want their children socialized into certain sets of values. They may want strict discipline for their child or to ensure that their child is in a safe environment, free of pupils who act out. If they are well-off enough, they may enter their children into an elite private school that will instill high expectations as well as preparation for elite colleges (Cookson and Persell, 1985).

Thirty-five years after Catholic education's high point in 1965, 85 percent of private school students are enrolled in religious schools (U.S. Department of Education, 2001). Most are still in Catholic establishments, whose enrollment is again rising. But many are now in Evangelical, Lutheran, or Jewish schools. Parents who send their children to religious schools generally do so because such schools provide a strong religious education that corresponds to their beliefs. True, a certain fraction of mainly inner-city children attend religious schools of a domination that does not correspond to their belief. Yet even they may be there as much for the socialization provided by strong, religious education as for better academics.

There are other grounds for believing that private schools might be organized in ways that make them very different from public schools. The market or religious hierarchies may push private school organizations to structure themselves differently from the way that they would be as public institutions. An autonomous, independent, secular private school is an organization unto itself, so we would expect it to do some things differently from a public school. Public schools may also be pushed to structure themselves differently from the way that they would be as autonomous organizations. If this is so, we need to see how much private schools are affected by market forces or religious hierarchies and how much public schools are affected by the public bureaucracy. We also need to examine how parents and teachers may behave differently with regard to schooling when they are in a market situation than when they send their children to the neighborhood public school.

Logically, in the 20 years since Coleman, Hoffer, and Kilgore (1982) published their study comparing private with public education, researchers should have figured out whether private schools organize themselves differently from public schools and whether these differences have a major impact on how much or what children learn. Researchers have certainly tried to model differences, but they have not been very successful in showing that the differences predicted by these models mean very much in making schools really different in terms of how much children learn.

In describing differences between private and public *secondary* schools, Coleman and his colleagues concluded that "In all of the private sectors, students take more academic subjects, and more advanced academic subjects than students in the public sector (except for the high performance public schools)" and that "Public schools, in general, are distinguished by their discipline problems" (Coleman et al., 1982, p. 120). They argue that this explains why students have higher academic achievement gains in Catholic schools and imply that there is something inherent about public and Catholic schools that creates these different conditions. Yet more students attend high-performance public schools in the United States than attend Catholic schools. Apparently, students in these public schools take the same number of (or more) advanced academic subjects as do students in private schools. They also perform as well or perhaps better in those subjects than students in Catholic schools.

This important caveat has plagued theorizing on public–private school differences. Many studies by organizational theorists in the 1980s and early 1990s tried to explain why private schools differ from public. But they did not agree and, despite much theorizing, never came up with convincing evidence that mapped out what these differences meant for school effectiveness or student achievement.

The essence of the problem is that public schools vary enormously and so do private schools. In addition, we would expect religious schools to be governed differently from secular, independent private schools and religious schools of different denominations to be governed differently. Some analysts have worried about such variation, but others have not. Furthermore, some analysts have tried to explain how and why private and public schools might have different organizations without drawing implications for school effectiveness, whereas others have plunged into predictions of differences in school effectiveness based on differences in school organization. The less the analysis is aware of variation within sectors, the more likely it is to be wrong.

What does all the theorizing tell us? The main theoretical argument is that, because the external contexts—the environment—of private and public schools differ, so do the internal features of private and public schools. In brief, this line of organizational theory argues that the *institution* of public schooling has developed a particular set of structures that shapes the organization of individual public schools. Private schools get their legitimacy as educational institutions from a different institutional environment and so should have a different organizational structure. For example, Stanford sociologists Richard Scott and John Meyer argue that "*some* of the differences in the internal organization between public and private schools can be attributed to differences in the structure of their environment" (Scott and Meyer, 1988, p. 129; italics added).

A public school takes in all comers. Teachers and the school principal are accountable to multiple constituencies, while needing to respond to the varying capabilities and needs of their students. Hence public schools have developed over time within a bureaucratic model operating under rational–legal norms. This is partly the result of government control, but is also due to the expectations of parents, businesses and other constituencies that demand accountability and legal protections (Talbert, 1988). Given its varied goals and constituencies, a public school's organization is bound to be complex and often subject to conflict. It also can appear incoherent because it tries to accomplish so many things at once. Scott and Meyer predict that organizations such as public schools, operating in "more complex and conflicted environments," will be necessarily more intricate administratively and have less coherent programs (1988, p. 129). They contend that "the involvement of the public schools in an environment with diverse pressures from so many organizational levels provides many resources for the public schools, but also immerses them in a complex and inconsistent controlling environment" (p. 159).

Although apparently similar in some aspects, Scott and Meyer argue that private schools can differ from their public counterparts in distinct ways. Private schools have to adhere somewhat to the public school "organizational model" in order to conform to legitimate or accepted norms and expectations of behavior (in addition, private schools are partially regulated by government). Furthermore, religious schools also draw on a traditional model of authority based on religious values of obedience and hierarchies within each religious order. Yet private schools are more likely to have a single objective and select (and be selected by) parents and their children who are in accord with that objective. A private school's organization should therefore be less complex and more aligned around a coherent program. "In sum, public, religious, and non-religious private schools are organizationally distinct because they gain legitimacy by being isomorphic with alternative models of authority and organization" (Talbert, 1988, p. 273).

Both Scott and Meyer and Talbert find some empirical evidence from a 1981 survey of hundreds of private and public schools to support these notions of organizational differences, but the results seem to suggest only that administrative differences exist due to different hierarchical regimes. They draw no conclusions about the relationship between these differences and student achievement. And most of the findings on less coherent programs refer to public middle and especially secondary schools, with their many tracks and multiple programs.

Bryk, Lee, and Holland (1993) continued in this same theoretical framework when they reanalyzed Catholic–public secondary differences a few years later. They also concluded that the differences between public and private sectors have their origins in different environments, but gave these environments a more historical–political cast. Catholic schools, especially Catholic secondary schools, were organized to help to create social mobility for a minority, discriminated-against group. They were also organized to reproduce a religious culture and, in many cities, to preserve various traditions imported from Catholic European countries. Because America's public education was, in principle, universal education, public schools were responsible not only for teaching students academic skills, but also for channeling students of various abilities into various tracks. According to Bryk, Lee, and Holland, Catholic secondary schools were able to focus on more narrow objectives for a more restricted constituency. This enabled them to create a clearer sense of purpose and community than public schools could. This, they claimed, has a significant positive effect on learning for low-income students.

To their credit, the Scott and Meyer, Talbert, and Bryk, Lee, and Holland studies recognized organizational variation *among* public and particularly among different types of private schools. They also recognized the difficulty of drawing too many conclusions from the organizational differences between the private and the public sector.[1]

Not so another set of environmental explanations that emphasizes the difference between government control of public schools and individual choice (*voluntarism*) in the private school sector. Salganik and Karweit (1982) supported the notion that government control makes public schools very different organizationally *and less effective* than private schools. They claim that, on the one hand, because parents and teachers *choose* private schools and the schools are self-governing, this assures consensus on school goals and high levels of commitment among each school's constituencies. On the other, government control, combined with conflicted goals and fragmented governance, legitimizes public schools, but promotes bureaucracy, disagreement among constituencies over values, little commitment by either teachers or parents, and low levels of effectiveness (Salganik and Karweit, 1982, pp. 153, 156).

Following Salganik and Karweit, Chubb and Moe (1990) focused on the rational–legal bureaucratic versus choice (voluntarism) environments for public and private schools. They promoted the idea that public schools were organized to serve bureaucratic needs rather than goals derived from the public interest or an inherently unequal social structure and that private schools were goal oriented and forced to respond to market competition (parent choice). Like Salganik and Karweit, they use an institutional perspective to flesh out Milton Friedman's argument against the inherent inefficiencies of public monopoly. And, like Friedman, they see the public school system as bureaucratic and political. To show that the institutional context of public schools really does shape the way that they behave, Chubb and Moe compare public school organizations with their private counterparts, which are situated in an allegedly different institutional context. Private schools, controlled "indirectly—by the marketplace," serve as a contrast to public schools, controlled by democratic politics.[2]

Because of the nature of these institutional settings—markets and politics—school organizations, Chubb and Moe (1990) claim, tend to be very different in private and public schools. The main differences are that private schools have a great deal more discretion in terms of choosing what they do and how they do it. They are free to adopt whatever practices they want in order to achieve the school's mission, as long as they attract a specialized clientele that values what they do. They also have an incentive to "take advantage of the expertise and judgment of [their] teachers" (p. 60). And they are less conflictual because of greater homogeneity of interests among parents, while their teachers and administrators are not accountable to hierarchical public bureaucracies.

On the other hand, Chubb and Moe (1990) characterize public educational practice as

> a world of rules imposed on the schools by local, state, and federal authorities . . . rules about curriculum, about instructional methods, about the design of special programs, about textbooks, about time spent on various activities, about what can and cannot be discussed. In addition, there are all sorts of rules—monitoring and reporting rules—designed to ensure that teachers are doing these things and not evading hierarchical control. . . . [These rules] cause [schools] to depart from what they might otherwise do, and thus to behave in ways that contradict or fail to take advantage of their professional judgment. (p. 59)

The main feature of Chubb and Moe's analysis is that it incorporates the underlying environmental analysis of the institutional organization theorists such as Scott and Meyer and Talbert, but ignores the discussions of differences between religious private schools and independent private schools. Chubb and Moe also downplay the possibility that many private schools are also subject to public regulation and the various warnings about variations in school autonomy within the public sector (e.g., differences between public schools with many federal and state programs and those with almost none).

Chubb and Moe's main contribution, however, is to link the broad brushstroke of organizational differences derived from markets versus bureaucracy, as applied to all private schools (market driven), and public schools (bureaucratically driven), to school effectiveness. In this linkage, large, suburban, high-performing public high schools are lumped in with small high-cost private academies, as well as with larger lower-cost urban and suburban Catholic high schools. Urban public high schools are the ones that largely appear at the other end of the spectrum.

Other models are not nearly so ready to accept this characterization of school differences. The organizational theorists make a good point that public schools are different from private schools in some of their underlying purposes, and this does affect how they are governed. Bryk and co-authors (1993) argue convincingly that Catholic educators made a conscious policy decision nearly a century ago not to put a vocational track in Catholic high schools. Coleman and co-authors (1982) are correct in arguing that multiple tracking is an important feature of America's public schools. Organizational theorists are probably right that tracking derives from the more complex demands placed on an accept-all-comers public system.

However, it may also have to do with the historical legacy of a society that has treated people of color differently from whites in their access to resources. Or it might also have to do with a class culture that divides up people in the educational system based on preconceptions of where they are supposed to end up in the labor market. Catholic schools may have avoided implementing some of these differential treatments to the same degree as public schools because of an expressed mission of promoting social mobility and cultural reproduction for Catholics. But it would be difficult to avoid classifying students in a mass education system differently from the way that the society as a whole has conventionally classified them. Indeed, a good case can be made that students are treated more equally in the public educational system than they are in the private business sector (Carnoy and Levin, 1985).

Some researchers argue that what and how much students learn vary more across social class groups than across schools organized by government or by religious groups or schools organized to appeal to particular nonreligious market niches. Almost 20 years ago, Jean Anyon studied five public schools in a New Jersey school district and showed wide differences in textbook choices and the way that these schools taught their pupils (Anyon, 1983). She argued that, in effect, the differences emerged from the different conceptions by both parents and teachers in each school of what was a good education. Furthermore, there seemed to be little disagreement between parents and teachers on this issue. Parents generally agreed that the school should teach what and in the way that the parents had learned. In these schools, conceptions of good schooling were related to parents' social class.

How would Chubb and Moe explain Anyon's findings? The schools she studied were all public schools, all prisoners of the same New Jersey school district bureaucracy. How could students in one school be taught a challenging, problem-based curriculum and students in a different, predominantly working-class school in the same district be taught from one textbook with factual questions and drill and kill exercises? Anyon suggests that the parents sending their children to each of these schools are satisfied with the curriculum and teaching styles; indeed, it is likely that, were they to send their children to private schools, they would choose schools similar to the public schools where their children were currently enrolled.

Other arguments also support the notion that private and public schools for different social class groups of students will not offer very different curricula or educational models. Economist Byron Brown (1992) theorizes that schooling is an uncertain business. Parents, striving to maximize the future life opportunities of their children, are naturally risk averse and tend to seek out schooling options that are tried and true. Experimentation with new pedagogical approaches or innovative curricular programs can turn out to be a high-stakes gamble with lasting effects; hence, parents, as well as private and public school educators, will drive their schools to act much like others. Brown argues that private establishments differentiate themselves from other educational offers not by breaking rank in the academic realm, but rather through offering special secondary services that do not affect labor market opportunities, such as religious instruction.

Brown's vision of how private and public schools organize themselves is set in a framework of individual families making value judgments about the quality of the education that their children receive, particularly in terms of how this education will enhance their children's life chances. Since the vast majority of parents are risk averters, especially since they know very little about the impact of one curriculum or another or one teaching method or another, they will generally insist on a conservative approach to schooling. A conservative approach means being not very different from the norm. So, rather than the innovativeness in curriculum and teaching predicted by Chubb and Moe, private schools will tend to be more conservative, sticking to structured, traditional teaching. On the other hand, in the absence of an incentive to cater to parents, according to this frame of analysis, public schools could well espouse a much greater variety of approaches.

If Anyon is right, various social class groups of parents have similar conceptions of what constitutes a good education based mainly on their own experience in school. But the conceptions vary across social class, not necessarily across school sectors. If Brown is right, then we should find that private and public schools offer similar academic schooling to each social-class group.

Anyon and Brown see a very different set of forces shaping school organization from that described by Chubb and Moe and sociologists such as Scott and Meyer or Talbert. There is no doubt that public high schools are more complex organizations than private high schools and that tracking is more likely to occur in public than private schools. These are important organizational differences. But private schools incorporate a much smaller proportion of students from the lowest three family income deciles. This alone could change how a school is organized and the kind of education offered.

Chubb and Moe test statistically for organizational differences in schools, but their results are derived from secondary data based on questionnaires given to school personnel, not direct observations in schools.[3] Yet, if their and Friedman's view of public schooling is correct, we should be able to observe obvious differences between public and private schools as they organize around bureaucratic or market-driven forces. Specifically, teachers and administrators in public schools should conceptualize accountability in rigid and bureaucratic terms, whereas teachers and administrators in private schools should lean toward parent and student demands.[4] If Anyon and Brown are correct, we should find small differences in what private and public schools do when they cater to similar groups of parents, but should find major differences across schools taking in children from different socioeconomic communities.

METHODOLOGY

What do you look for when you study a school? You can observe teachers teaching and administrators administering and, if you stay in the school long enough, you can get a sense of what and how students learn. It is fairly easy to tell the difference between a very well run school with very good teachers and a poorly organized school with highly disorganized teachers. But most teachers and schools are not at the extremes. Differences among most schools are not always obvious.

In thinking about how we would study schools to disentangle the less obvious differences, we searched for variables that would reveal schools' objectives and how *coherently* schools' staff organized their work around these objectives. So we wanted measures of what school personnel and parents felt *accountable for* and how well their work reflected this accountability. We developed a relatively simple working theory of school *internal accountability.*[5] The theory is based on the premise that schools actually have conceptions of accountability embedded in the patterns of their day-to-day operations and that a school's conception of accountability significantly influences how it delivers education. We assume that schools must solve the problem of accountability in some way in order to function and that the way that it solves this problem is reflected in the way teachers, administrators, students, and parents talk about the fundamental issues of schooling. We also assume that formal, external accountability systems, such as state or district bureaucracies or market forces, are only one among many factors that influence a school's internal sense of accountability.

Schools form their conceptions of accountability from a variety of sources, including individual teachers' and administrators' beliefs about teaching and learning, their shared understandings of who their students are, the routines that they develop for getting their work done, and external expectations from parents, communities, and the administrative agencies under which they work. To capture this construction of accountability, our theory posits a relationship among three tiers: (1) the individual's sense of accountability, or *responsibility;* (2) the collective sense of accountability of parents, teachers, administrators, and students, or *expectations;* and (3) the organizational rules, incentives, and implementation mechanisms that constitute the *formal accountability* system in schools. These accountability mechanisms represent the variety of ways, formal and informal, in which people in schools (including parents, in some cases) *give an account* of their actions to someone in a position of formal authority inside or outside the school. Mechanisms are *formal* when they are recorded in a policy handbook or are part of a union contract. *Informal* mechanisms refer to a set of measures that school actors respond to, regardless of what bureaucratic rules and regulations in fact say; they are organic to the particular school culture. Mechanisms can also vary in their consequences for success or failure. They can be *low stakes,* resulting only in approval or disapproval by, say, the principal. Or they can be *high stakes,* involving public disclosure or financial sanctions and rewards.

Accountability mechanisms are what most people, including Friedman and Chubb and Moe, envisage when they discuss bureaucracy and markets. Teachers in public schools are characterized as subject to complex *formal* accountability mechanisms requiring adherence to bureaucratic rules and regulations that have little to do with maximizing pupils' academic performance. The principal of a public school is characterized as enforcing these externally imposed mechanisms. The market is also an accountability mechanism, and an allegedly *high-stakes* one, since failure to conform to market signals implies loss of clientele. It is not clear whether bureaucratic mechanisms are high or low stakes. Most critics of public schooling claim, on the one hand, that school bureaucracies spend their time enforcing rules and regulations. On the other hand, teacher labor unions are often described as able to blunt any attempts to sanction teachers who do not conform to these rules. This would suggest that public schools are organized around complex, bureaucratic (external), *low-stakes* accountability mechanisms. Yet, in recent years, there has been a strong and continuous tendency to increase the stakes in schooling services provision through mandated district-, state-, and now national-accountability standards and performance incentive schemes.

In our working theory, responsibility, expectations, and accountability operate in a mutual relationship with each other. This relationship varies from school to school. A given school's response to the problem of accountability is a product of how it resolves the conflicts and complementarities among individuals' internalized notions of accountability, their shared expectations, and formal and informal mechanisms that push them to account to someone else for what they do. Schools are likely to have more operative internal accountability systems if their formal and informal mechanisms are *aligned with* individuals' internalized notions of accountability (responsibility) and collective expectations of the school (Abelmann and Elmore, 1999). At the other extreme, a high degree of incoherence among the three levels of accountability translates into a relatively weak or dysfunctional internal accountability system. This would be the case, for example, cited by Chubb and Moe, when a principal forces teachers to adhere to rules that they know result in poor academic outcomes.

Schools not only vary in the degree of alignment between the different levels of accountability, but also on *what* they consider themselves to be accountable for. A school can exhibit a high degree of alignment around student academic achievement, or it may organize itself around order and discipline in the classrooms, with little or no coherence to academic goals. As some of our case studies suggest, just because a school exhibits a high degree of alignment does not mean that it is aligned around academic objectives.

DATA

Along with a team from Harvard University's Graduate School of Education, our team at Stanford University originally studied a highly diverse sample of twenty-five schools, roughly half located in a major metropolitan area on the East Coast and roughly half in two metropolitan areas on the West Coast. The Stanford–Harvard sample represented public, private, and charter elementary, middle, and high schools. Private schools included both parochial and independent establishments. We also targeted schools within each sector (private, public, or charter) that served different social-class populations. In every school, we spent time in classrooms and interviewed teachers, administrators, parents, and, in a few cases, students.

For the purpose of this study, we decided to expand our sample on the West Coast and focus only on primary and middle schools. We had learned from the East Coast case studies, but had only visited one of the schools personally. We omitted the high schools from the study because we had too few of them. By the time we finished interviewing, we had been in sixteen West Coast primary and middle schools.

The sixteen schools examined in this study are located in large metropolitan areas. In all cases, interview subjects were assured confidentiality and anonymity. For this reason, all school and individual names used here, are pseudonyms. A brief description of each school in our sample follows:

Adams Charter Middle School was started by parents in 1994. Adams' charter requires that the school abide by all the provisions set out in the California Education Code, giving it many characteristics of a traditional public school. The school is located in a suburban community, and its seventy-five seventh- and eighth-grade students are mostly from upper-middle-class families. Parents supplement the school budget with monthly pledges. The average annual pledge is $702 per child. Thus, while we categorize this as one of the public schools in our study, it could arguably be considered a private school.

Ayacucho Elementary School is a Title I public school that enrolls approximately 450 students in grades K to 5. It is located in a low-income urban area that, by historical accident, is on the outskirts of, and within, an affluent suburban school district. About half of the school's students are Latino, and a small percentage are Asian or African American. Ayacucho operates both a bilingual and an English educational program at each grade level.

Madison Charter School was selected by the county's board of supervisors to become a charter school in 1994 because it had consistently produced the lowest achievement scores in its district. Madison enrolls nearly 600 K to 6 students. The school population largely consists of recent Mexican immigrants who live in the immediate vicinity. Only a few children from the neighboring, predominantly white, affluent community attend Madison. Its academic program emphasizes a longer school year, and parents must sign a contract to volunteer in the school for 4 hours a month. In addition, Madison operates a preschool on the premises, although preschool enrollments are low because fees are charged on a sliding scale that many parents consider too expensive.

Mashita Middle School enrolls 1,700 students. It has a predominantly minority student body, drawn historically from families of longshoremen and other port workers, who dominate its harbor community. School officials are troubled by a community culture that assumes that good jobs will be available to young people who do not have a good education. This mostly stable working-class community, however, is undergoing significant demographic changes.

United Primary School is situated in a lower- to middle-income area of a large city. It enrolls 710 K to 5 students, three-quarters of whom are eligible for free or reduced-price lunches and half of whom are limited-English proficient. A district-wide desegregation court order requires that no more than 45 percent of the school's students can be of one racial or ethnic group. Thus, United is roughly 31 percent Chinese, 28 percent Latino, 15 percent African American, 12 percent Filipino, 9 percent "other non-white," and 4 percent "other white." Because of its Spanish and Chinese bilingual programs, however, many classrooms do not reflect the school's diversity. The school also attempts to integrate health, social, educational, financial, legal and other support services for the whole family.

Olympic Charter School was originally a magnet school. Despite its charter status, this K to 5 public school of 385 students has remained financially fully integrated with its urban school district. In addition, Olympic heavily depends on parent and corporate fund raising to supplement the per-pupil allotment that the school receives from the school district. Its academic program emphasizes an explicit constructivist educational philosophy.

Renaissance Middle School is a public school that, because of consistently low student achievement, was reconstituted by the district superintendent in 1994 with an entirely new faculty and staff. Located in a low-income community with substantial public housing, Renaissance's student body reflects its neighborhood's demography and is primarily comprised of ethnic minorities. Three-quarters of the student body qualifies for free or reduced-price lunches.

Tatuna Point Elementary School enrolls 560 K to 6 students. It is located in a high-income suburban community where many parents are professionals, businesspeople, and corporate executives. Parents can log a total of 8,000 volunteer hours during the school year. The student body is largely white or Asian. Average test scores are above the 90th percentile on nationally normed standardized tests. Most children are expected not only to attend college, but to attend elite institutions of higher education. A parent-run educational foundation raised $130,000 in the past year. The funds were destined for the hiring of two full-time resource teachers and six part-time paraprofessionals to supplement the regular staff hired from district funds. The PTA donated an additional $50,000 for computers and playground equipment.

Knuckleborough Private School is a for-profit K to 8 school of 360 students situated in the heart of a low- to middle-income neighborhood. The student body, however, is predominantly white and middle class. Tuition fees amount to approximately $5,000 annually. For an additional fee, parents have access to extended-care services (from 7:00 A.M. to 6:30 P.M.). A major challenge faced by this school is a teacher turnover rate exceeding 40 percent per year. This is largely an outcome of low salaries (average teacher salary of $24,000). Students, on the other hand, are the mainstay of the school, many spending a full 9 years at Knuckleborough.

Liniers French School is a private independent school of 350 students that provides an immersion-based bilingual and multicultural education to students from prekindergarten through seventh grade. The student body is 61 percent French, 32 percent American, and 7 percent international. Liniers is located in an affluent suburb, and the annual tuition rate is approximately $9,500. The school has a rigorous academic program, but it must engage in a balancing act to satisfy the competing demands from its two primary clienteles, which push school officials to devote more attention to and concentrate their efforts on either the American or the French aspects of the curricula.

Shalom Ieladim Jewish School was founded in 1990. This private day school of grades K to 5 serves families of reform, reconstructionist, conservative, orthodox, and unaffiliated backgrounds. It is located in an affluent suburb and has an annual tuition rate of $6,950. The Jewish Community Federation provides an additional subsidy of $850 per student per year. In an attempt to remain diverse, the school allocates about 20 percent of its budget to need-based scholarships for those who cannot afford full tuition. About one-quarter of the school's 150 students has emigrated from Israel or Russia. Most parents are professionals in the service or technology industries. All students are Jewish, but some academic teachers are not. The school's academic program is complemented with extensive Judaic and Hebrew studies.

St. Barbara's Catholic School is located in an inner suburb. This K to 8 private school of 600 students has a competitive admissions process. Approximately half of all kindergarten applicants gain admission every year. Transfer students may be accepted on an occasional basis to fill any vacancies provided that they test at grade level. St. Barbara's selective enrollment process allows it to have a student body that is somewhat less impoverished and minority than its surrounding community. The school staff is exclusively comprised of lay educators, with the exception of the principal.

St. Donat's Catholic School is operated by a Dominican Sisters order in conjunction with the local archdiocese. It serves about 230 students, about 70 percent Latino, in grades K through 8. The faculty consists of three Dominican nuns and eight lay teachers, with another Dominican sister as part-time special needs coordinator. Most parents work in service jobs like waitressing, janitorial services, cooking, accounting, insurance, and minibus driving. Annual tuition is $2,350. With an operating cost of $2,800 per pupil, the school devotes great effort to fund-raising events and seeking foundation grants. Rising real estate values in the surrounding community result in continuing enrollment losses, as the families who have traditionally enrolled their children at St. Donat's move away to more affordable areas.

St. Felipe's Catholic School is also operated by Dominican Sisters. Located in the heart of the inner city, St. Felipe's caters to 290 students. About half of the student body is non-Catholic. The principal, a Dominican nun, is the only member of the religious order on the faculty. St. Felipe's Parish has undergone a tumultuous period. In the early 1990s, it was the site of riots. In the period that ensued, the community has changed rapidly, from mostly African American to mostly Latino. Enrollment, drawn almost entirely from the surrounding parish, is now 70 percent African American and 30 percent Latino. Nearly 40 percent of students live with single parents and another 7 percent live with grandparents. St. Felipe's offers a morning care program beginning at 6:00 A.M. and an afterschool program until 6:00 P.M. Tuition is $2,500 a year, with a discounted plan available for parents who engage in fund-raising activities. The archdiocese provides twenty-six students with scholarships of $600 each.

St. Jeremy's Lutheran School is found within the same inner suburban community as St. Barbara's Catholic School. This is a K to 8 school serving 206 students. As the surrounding community becomes predominantly Latino, few parish families have school-aged children any more. Only eight parishioner children were enrolled during the 1996–1997 school year. Nonetheless, the school has retained a strong religious focus. St. Jeremy's operates under complete autonomy from higher church bodies. A parish-elected board is responsible for selecting the principal, interviewing teacher candidates, and reviewing all major curricular and other school policies. The staff is comprised entirely of graduates of the Missouri Synod's Concordia College system or of equivalent religious training. One educator is an ordained Lutheran minister. While this case study was being conducted, St. Jeremy's was riven by policy disputes between the school board, the pastor, the principal, and the faculty. Unable to resolve these, the school closed at the end of the 1997–1998 school year.

St. Milton's Catholic School is a K to 8 school located in the same riot-impacted community as St. Felipe's Catholic School. A significant number of St. Milton's 220 students, however, come from families who moved away to more suburban communities as the parish demographics changed. Many parents are St. Milton's graduates themselves. Nonetheless, attrition rates are high. Out of thirty-five students, only six eighth-graders had been in the school since kindergarten. Tuition fees range from $1,625 for parishioners' children to $1,975 for non-Catholic students. The principal must frequently engage in extensive tuition negotiations with families in financial difficulty. Fund raising is a major source of concern for school administrators.

One critique of a study that uses cases, rather than a large, random sample of schools, is that we have not chosen a representative set of schools and hence cannot draw conclusions regarding either accountability systems or possible differences or similarities between private and public schools. It is true that our sample is not randomly selected. It was drawn to represent a range of possible variation, rather than as distributionally representative of the population of schools. It is also true that we can say nothing concerning high schools, since we decided not to study that level. But by visiting a reasonably substantial number of public and private schools catering to higher and lower socioeconomic background students in two metropolitan areas, we should be able to find the kinds of differences in accountability systems claimed by market advocates. Their claim, after all, is that market-driven behavior is *observably* and *significantly* different from bureaucratically driven behavior. If this is the case, such differences should be observable in a sample of sixteen schools. If they are not observable in this sample, then it is really up to market advocates to show what it is about our schools that would produce this result.

Two interviewers went to each school and recorded interviews with parents, teachers, and administrators. They also observed teachers teaching in classrooms before and after interviews. Interviewers conducted their field research over a number of school visits and, in some cases, interviewed teachers and administrators more than once. Each interview was transcribed and, based on the interviews, each school was written up as a case study. We used the case studies, as well as the backup interviews, for the analysis that we present here.

We are very aware that qualitative analysis of this type is subject to interpretation. Qualitative research can focus on some points that school personnel and parents make and ignore other points. It is also possible to miss the point altogether. Yet, as quantitative researchers, we also know how easy it is to manipulate quantitative data. While the National Center of Educational Statistics collected data on a random sample of schools, researchers using these data have come to very different conclusions, as we showed in the previous chapter.

So our qualitative study is an effective way to check on those impressive quantitative analyses. Through a semistructured interview protocol, teachers, administrators, and parents shared candidly their impressions about key issues in each school. Their openness enabled us, we believe, to capture the essence of these schools and, in turn, to understand patterns of organization, the nature of what went on in classrooms, the objectives of each school's accountability system, and its coherence.

In the chapters that follow, we will try to give you the flavor of the schools we visited and convince you that what we saw there fits particular patterns. Are private schools all that different from public schools? Let's take a look.

[3]

STUDENT ACHIEVEMENT
AND CLIENT ORIENTATION
IN PUBLIC AND PRIVATE SCHOOLS

Since the mid-1950s, when Milton Friedman revived the idea that government should not administer education,[1] many social scientists have espoused the view that public schools are inherently inefficient. They claim that privately run schools can provide services more effectively. The most important of this argument's many parts is that a publicly run system restricts parents' choice and that, without fair competition, public schools do not have to be responsive or accountable to parents' demands. Friedman argued that, by giving parents the possibility of sending their children to any school that met minimum standards, parents could "express their views about schools directly, by withdrawing their children from one school and sending them to another, to a much greater extent than is now possible" and that "here, as in other fields, competitive private enterprise is likely to be far more efficient in meeting consumer demands than either nationalized enterprises or enterprises run to serve other purposes" (Friedman, 1955, p. 129).

For Friedman, public schools are inefficient because nothing *makes* them be efficient, at least in terms of delivering the kinds of services that parents want. Public schools do not have to compete on the same ground with other schools that might deliver more and better education. And with a "monopoly" in neighborhood education, public schools are likely to produce education in a way that serves purposes other than parent wishes.

In *Policy, Markets, and America's Schools,* John Chubb and Terry Moe argue that in a democratic society the "public will" is the outcome of negotiation and compromise among competing special-interest groups with conflicting interests. This process shackles public education into a bureaucratic process in which the voices of parents go unheard. Instead of being held prisoners to governmental politics, school choice would give parents the option to transfer their children from one school to another and vote with their feet. The market, according to Chubb and Moe, will allow schools to fashion themselves "in response to what parents and students want" (Chubb and Moe, 1990, p. 212).

Current debates over school choice have been fueled by the presumed ability of private schools to serve clients with a more adaptive organization than public schools (see, e.g., Kirkpatrick, 1990). Conservative groups, together with Catholic and other religious groups, have become increasingly vocal advocates for vouchers. They contend that the time has come to break the monopoly on education held by public schooling and make public funding for private schools available. School choice advocates argue that privatization and vouchers are means that will make schools more accountable to parents, particularly to low-income families, who finally would have a say as to where their children will go to school (Finn, 1990). Chester Finn, former deputy secretary of education under President Reagan, conveyed with the following words the power of voucher programs to equalize educational opportunities for low-income parents: "We don't tell poor people what to eat; we give them food stamps. We don't tell them which doctor to go to; they have Medicaid cards. [Yet, in education, only the rich can] buy their way out, by moving into a certain neighborhood or choosing a private school" (Wallis, 1994, p. 57).

If we assume that market-driven educational models as propounded by Friedman and others after him are correct, we would expect to observe striking differences between public and private schools with regard to their client orientation. Since public schools in these models are steered by bureaucratic principles, we would expect to find that public schools are less responsive to parental demands than private schools. Because private schools depend on consumer satisfaction for their survival, they are expected to be more responsive to parental demands than public institutions. Schools that are not in touch with the needs of parents and students would theoretically be eventually forced out of the market. Public schools, on the other hand, have fewer incentives to respond to parental concerns for two reasons: parents and students are a captive constituency, and parental expectations are only one of a large number of competing demands that public schools confront.

The data from our sample of schools challenges the accuracy of these assertions. We were not able to observe any such systematic differences. The empirical evidence that we collected suggests a different conceptualization. The first section in this chapter explores the difficulties in involving parents in academic matters in both public and private schools within lower-income communities. Parents tend to be largely detached from schools, and teachers must face the challenge of securing parental support to accomplish their academic objectives. Private and charter schools are increasingly resorting to mandating parental participation to bring parents closer to schools. On the other hand, the second section illustrates how both private and public schools are held very much accountable by parents in higher-income communities. These parents tend to be active participants in school affairs and do not hesitate to communicate their wishes and concerns to school staff. The third section underscores that, contrary to the precepts of market-driven educational models, it is private schools that have proved to be more successful in containing parental voice and demands for change. As public institutions, public schools have an obligation to respond to their constituency. Instead, private establishments can shield behind their stated missions and operational objectives. The final section challenges the notion that markets necessarily drive private schools toward a stronger academic orientation. In lower-income communities, parental choices are equally or more driven by nonacademic concerns such as school safety, discipline, or religious education.

PARENTAL INVOLVEMENT IN LOWER-INCOME SCHOOLS[2]

Parental participation in a child's education is usually considered a key element for making high student achievement possible. Education is a joint production that requires mutual support and reinforcement from teachers and parents.

All the schools in our sample, private and public alike, display similar organizational channels to encourage parental participation. Most schools have parent–teacher organizations that are in charge of voicing parental issues and regular parent–teacher conferences that allow families to raise matters of concern. At the beginning of every year, teachers invite parents into their classroom and request their assistance in performing clerical and administrative duties, supporting pedagogical exercises, or taking part in field trips and special schoolwide events. Both public and private schools ask parents to donate a certain number of volunteer work-hours in various school activities as a means to bring parents closer to schools and also to help to defray the costs of schooling.

Our school case studies reveal that often instructional staff perceive their greatest problem to be lack of parental involvement in their children's education. Schools where these grievances were most frequent were low-income schools, both public and private.

Administrators and principals complained frequently that too few parents volunteered in classrooms, attended meetings to discuss school policy or children's progress, or paid sufficient attention to the importance of homework. When teachers and principals in low-income schools were asked what they wanted to change most, they all said, irrespective of the source of their funding, that they wished for greater parental participation. Routine parental involvement in homework and other academic support was more an exception than the rule, a subject of great faculty frustration.

Educators emphasize that parental disengagement has direct consequences on educational outcomes. For example, an upper-grade teacher at St. Donat's, a parochial school located in a low-income community of largely Central American immigrants, directly attributed the poor academic achievement of her students to lack of parental support and involvement in the schooling of their children: "[Students] could perform much, much better, but there's nobody after school hours to help them. . . . You'd hope that the parents would understand the importance of their role in the education of their kids." The vice-principal at another low-income Catholic school suggested that the lack of parental involvement in academic matters was a reflection of a more diffused disposition toward academic achievement in a low-income environment: "I think part of [the parental disengagement in schooling] may be their culture, too. Education is maybe not the very top, top, top priority on their list. They want the children to be obedient, to behave, to be polite and such. But education is not, because of maybe their background, education is not always their top priority."

The levels of parental participation among lower-income public and private schools varied to some extent. Some schools were more successful than others in getting parents to increase their involvement. St. Barbara's, an elementary Catholic school serving a middle to lower middle-income, inner-ring suburb, offers an edifying example. St. Barbara's involves parents in instructional as well as fund-raising activities. They are required to attend schoolwide meetings (or be expected to pay a "fine" for being absent) and to volunteer a minimum of 25 hours per year for a variety of administrative or classroom activities. In addition, St. Barbara's requires each family to purchase an *agenda book,* a colorful and attractively illustrated booklet that includes school rules, health tips, and other relevant information. The book includes weekly calendars with space for students to fill in their daily assignments and to record their completion, plus space for parents to sign, indicating supervision of homework. Teachers frequently check for parents' signatures, and the principal walks through the classrooms every week to inspect each child's agenda book.

St. Barbara's also prescribes parent involvement with a policy of requiring all parents of children in grades K to 3, without exception, to come to the classroom at the end of the school day to meet their children. There is a $1 per minute fine for parents who are late. This policy not only assures that teachers will not be detained at school caring for young children whose parents are tardy, but also structures a situation in which teachers can talk to any parent whose child the teacher believes would benefit from such a discussion.

Parents are also expected to provide explicit support in academic matters. St. Barbara's first-grade parents are required to read to their first-grade children for a minimum of 15 minutes each evening. Parents must sign and send to the teacher a *reading card,* testifying that they have accomplished this goal. Teachers report that they are careful to verify that these cards have been signed.

This approach has seemed to work well for St. Barbara's, and most teachers suggest that they have been able to develop an ongoing relationship with each parent and secure their support in their child's academic progress. However, the school was able to implement this policy successfully only in the lower grades.

Some low-income public schools have also demonstrated success in encouraging parental involvement and participation in the academic program. United Primary School is a Title I public school operating under a desegregation order. One-third of the student body is Chinese, one-third Latino, and one-sixth white, while other minorities comprise the balance.[3] About 40 percent of the parents actively participate in school activities on a regular basis, not only in administrative duties, but also in regular classroom work, parenting classes, or academic events like "math night."

Several unique features of the school probably contribute to its high degree of parental participation. First, there is a deliberate effort to integrate parents into the school. PTA meetings are conducted in English, Spanish, and Chinese, and the school hires parent coordinators for each of these language groups. Teachers attempt to create homework assignments that involve the child's entire family. If a child is having either academic or behavioral difficulty, the school assembles a *school study team* on which the academic staff, school nurse, and other social service providers join with the child's parents to review the student's strengths and weaknesses and make recommendations for home behavioral changes. Through this process, parents and school staff members attempt to become mutually responsible for the student's improvement.

Second, family social services, including financial, legal, health, and immigration services, are coordinated and delivered from the school site. A neighborhood community center works collaboratively with the school to provide parenting classes, adult literacy classes, and child care. Thus, the school plays a role not only as an academic institution, but also as a neighborhood service center.

A poll of parents several years ago determined that they wanted United to state its mission as preparing every child for college. Not all teachers were quick to embrace this college-bound vision for all students, but the principal recounted that, when there was resistance to this goal, she asked teachers in turn "what *they* aspired for their own children." The school, in the end, agreed to adopt the college-bound mission.

In contrast, other schools that apparently put as much effort into parent recruitment were not so fortunate. One teacher at St. Donat's, for instance, told us that she rarely hears from parents, and "when I do, the parents I do hear from, their child is doing okay. And the ones I don't hear from, those are the ones who are harder to get in touch with. . . . I find that the child who has the most problems, their parents usually are not involved." At St. Milton's, another Catholic school located in an inner-city African-American community, teachers regretted the fact that parents left all instructional matters in the hands of the school, to the frustration of teachers wanting parents to be more involved.

Student behavioral issues, rather than a concern for academic achievement, seem to exert a stronger pull for parents to voice their opinions and defend their children's right to schooling. Parental unwillingness to defer to school disciplinary decisions appears to be a common phenomenon in contemporary schools, private and public alike. St. Felipe's is a parochial school in the same cachement area as St. Milton's. Here the faculty described parents as more involved, but too often in order to protect their sons or daughters from academic or behavioral disciplinary admonishments.

Similarly, at Mashita Middle School, a public school, the principal noted that an increasing share of her time and attention is devoted to handling complaints from parents who question disciplinary decisions of teachers or administrators. The Mashita principal described this dilemma in the following way:

> I think it's critical to have parent involvement but . . . we've almost . . . gone too far . . . when we think that parents can challenge every decision that we make. We are questioned all of the time in a fashion that I don't see as productive. When, for example, I make a decision and a child's

parents challenge me, I give them a very good explanation of why it was done . . . but they want it their way. So the first thing they do is call my supervisor, and maybe my supervisor's supervisor. That kind of thing is counterproductive. We've spent way too much emotion and energy in dealing with . . . overpermissiveness . . . and we need to be able, in the public schools, to say, "This is not right, we have these rules. Yes, it's a public school and we want you here, but when you do that, you can't be part of the school situation."

The voice found by parents at Mashita to express opposition to disciplinary decisions finds no match in other realms. The Mashita principal reported that parents almost never challenge faculty professional judgments on curricular or instructional issues. In fact, the opposite problem, too much parental passivity, prevails. The principal and faculty members interviewed complained that their instructional effectiveness was limited by the failure of parents to be engaged. In a poll of Mashita faculty, lack of parental support and involvement in the academic program was named the school's most serious problem. The faculty made reference to inadequate parent involvement in supervising homework, in setting standards regarding the importance of academic work, and in communicating to their children that they should come to school prepared.

In both public and private schools located in lower-income and lower–middle class communities, we found teachers making strong efforts to increase parental awareness on academic matters, often to little avail. St. Jeremy's Lutheran School serves a lower–middle class working community. There are few formal requirements for parental involvement beyond paying tuition. One expectation is that twice a year parents will personally come to school to receive their children's report cards from the teachers. In addition, the school makes other efforts to keep parents informed about academic issues. Teachers are expected to send home a weekly newsletter describing class assignments. The principal himself frequently prods teachers if the newsletter is not produced on time.

Lay democratic control is a feature of the Lutheran synod to which St. Jeremy's belongs. Yet, because only church members are eligible to serve on school governing boards and because few parents are members of the church, only a small number of parents are eligible to participate. As an alternative, the school established a monthly *parent forum* whose meetings can be attended by all parents without distinction. The school hopes that parents will provide input about policy and become more informed about academic and other school policies. School administrators and teachers, however, have expressed great frustration, because they have not succeeded in attracting significant numbers of parents to these meetings.

At Mashita Middle School, a teacher remarked that she devotes one conference period a week to telephoning parents, but she laments she gets little constructive response. According to this instructor, some parents are not concerned if their child is getting a D, because they consider this to be a passing grade. Other parents become hostile if the teacher reports that their child is not doing well and they blame her for the student's poor performance. Likewise, another Mashita teacher described programming the school's automatic computer phone dialer with a message trying to reach out to at least ten students undergoing academic difficulties per month. The teacher protested that, throughout the entire year, she had received only one phone call back in response. As part of an Annenberg Foundation restructuring grant, Mashita Middle School established a focus group of parents and teachers to develop ways to increase parent involvement of the supportive type that teachers consider important. The group developed plans for parent training, but there was almost no parental response and the group disbanded.

While lack of parent involvement was a commonly voiced complaint among educators at Mashita Middle School, the faculty of a demographically similar public school, Ayacucho Elementary, rarely raised the issue. The difference, however, is not attributable to the greater involvement of Ayacucho parents. Instead, the Ayacucho faculty expected little from the school's low-income Latino immigrant parents with little formal education. Overall, parents at Ayacucho express satisfaction with the school's academic outcomes. Parents' expectations are frequently limited to a hope that the school will be successful in motivating their children to continue their education into high school. In contrast, faculty members are distressed about low test scores and voice complaints about the school's lack of consistent high standards.

At Ayacucho, parents are required to meet twice a year with their child's teacher, once at the beginning of the year to establish goals and once at the end to assess progress. This process has been established to secure support from the parent community to raise student achievement. But this effort has rendered little fruit. Teachers are convinced that the chances for academic advancement of these children rest squarely on their teachers' shoulders.

How much teachers can do to enhance academic achievement in the absence of sustained parental involvement has become an important issue at Renaissance Middle School, a low-income public school that was reconstituted by its large urban school district because of a pattern of low test scores. The new principal hired an almost entirely new staff, based on the candidates' dedication to the conviction that "all students can learn." Yet the new staff has experienced high turnover since reconstitution. One of several reasons for teacher burnout has been the administration's and teachers' efforts to improve academic outcomes without parental support. One teacher explained that, in a normal school, a good teacher would try to meet a student "halfway," with the student's half being the motivation and support that he or she brings from home. At Renaissance, the teacher said, teachers attempt to go "ninety percent of the way." Another instructor complained that parents expect teachers to reform behavior that results from a lack of discipline at home. And according to another teacher, parents treat the school as a "baby-sitting center" where they can drop children off in the morning and pick them up in the afternoon or evening without being concerned about what happens in between.

These frustrations among Renaissance teachers echo those of teachers in private schools. In the case of St. Donat's, many parents do not speak English. Because the school has no bilingual program or bilingual staff, involving parents meaningfully in the educational program is not a feasible school ambition. In this, as in other low-income private schools, parent volunteerism is mostly restricted to occasional chaperoning of field trips, fund raising, maintaining school facilities, and performing administrative duties.

There is some evidence that parents resent the schools' frequent appeals for volunteerism, fund raising, and demands for support of their children's academic efforts. As one St. Milton's parent put it, "every time you turn around, there's something that needs selling"—candy, raffles, and the like. But while parents were resentful of these demands for involvement, teachers at these schools were equally unhappy that parent participation was so limited. Teachers frequently complained that some parents felt that, having paid tuition, they had done their share, and it was up to the school to make education successful. A teacher at St. Donat's explained that parents, overall, delegate the responsibility for their children's education entirely to the school and are vexed by the periodic appeals for assistance: parents "resent the school because they feel that we should be able to do everything. They shouldn't have to do anything. They're paying us to take care of all these things."

Low-income schools are increasingly mandating parental participation as a strategy to bring parents closer to schools. Private schools have an advantage in procuring parental involvement because they can make it a condition for student enrollment. Requirements for parental volunteerism is usually part of the parent contract. In other words, parents must agree to contribute a certain number of hours of their time per month in the school. Not uncommonly, principals found it difficult to enforce compliance with this provision. At St. Milton's, for example, parents are expected to donate 30 hours per year to the school. Only some parents actually fulfill this requirement, and many utilize the option to make additional financial contributions instead of performing. Most schools have a policy permitting parents to buy back their service commitments by making additional financial contributions in lieu of volunteering.

Madison Charter School is a public school of mostly poor immigrant Latino children. The school was converted to charter status not in response to parental pressure, but rather by a local school district hoping to boost Madison's very low mean achievement scores (in the bottom quartile on standardized tests). In fact, the conversion took place over the initial objections of most Latino parents, who suspected that the charter might take away their community public school. The theory behind the charter, however, was that academic performance would improve if the school were more accountable to parents.

Parents make up half of Madison's board of directors, and the school, like other private or charter schools that we studied, requires parents to make a monthly volunteer commitment. Parents can fulfill this obligation by helping in classes, performing clerical or custodial work, attending governing board or schoolwide meetings (the most common form of participation), or taking English language classes themselves. The school's *parent contract* also requires parents to send children to school on time, to observe the school uniform policy, and to check student work folders once a week. Madison has a full-time staff member assigned to helping parents to fulfill their 4-hour monthly commitment. Yet, despite these efforts, parental participation has increased only moderately, and the faculty believes that the level of parental support remains insufficient. Goals for test score improvement have not been met, and test results are barely higher than the low precharter level that provoked conversion to charter status in the first place.

An important distinction must be drawn between this kind of mandated parental involvement and school client orientation. Mandating parental engagement in school or classroom activities is not necessarily a measure of school responsiveness to parental demands. On the contrary, schools themselves often dictate the terms of parental participation. In most low-income schools that we observed, while great effort was expended to attempt to increase parental collaboration, this effort was most frequently directed to enlisting parents in fund-raising endeavors and only secondarily to getting them involved in academic support activities or encouraging them to voice their opinions. Involvement in the academic program was a rare way of meeting mandated participation requirements, both because parents did not have the skills or confidence to support the educational program and because the school pressed them to fulfill their commitments by engaging in school maintenance, not academic, volunteerism.

Parents often do not participate in school activities out of their own accord or take the initiative to express their concerns or make demands. Rather, parents are largely drawn in by the school, and they act to some extent as its "guests." Their responsibility is circumscribed to putting into practice the school's own educational directives. They largely do not operate as independent actors that can hold the school accountable for academic outcomes.

In summary, despite efforts to *involve* parents in academic matters, low-income schools cannot be said to have fostered a sense of *accountability* to parents over academic achievement in a meaningful sense. The motor behind parental involvement comes primarily from the school and district professional staff, not from parents themselves. Parental presence in school affairs remains largely organized and regulated by the school professional staff. These schools, in fact, are not accountable to parents; rather, they attempt in a sense to make parents accountable to the school.

PARENTAL INVOLVEMENT IN HIGHER-INCOME SCHOOLS

There is a striking difference when we observed parental behavior in schools in higher-income neighborhoods. Administrators and teachers had the opposite complaint than their counterparts in low-income locales: too much parental involvement. School faculty argued that parents interfered too frequently in curricular matters, that they had uninformed preconceptions about proper pedagogical or disciplinary practice, and that they exhibited a lack of respect for the professional competence of the instructional staff. This was the case in both private and public schools, where parents felt confident that they knew best what a proper education entailed and were without compunction to communicate this to teachers and administrative staff.

But our case studies also indicate that there is an important distinction in the client orientation of public and private establishments. The differences observed in the role of parents in both types of educational establishments challenge the expectation that public schools are not held accountable by their customers. Furthermore, our data call into question the widely held assumption that private schools are necessarily more responsive to their clientele than government-run schools. This is the subject to which we now turn our attention.

PARENTAL INVOLVEMENT IN UPPER-INCOME PRIVATE SCHOOLS

"The school does not exist to serve parents"

Highly educated parents who are the typical clientele of elite private schools often feel that they have the right to intercede in educational decisions. School administrators and teachers tend to exhibit resistance to parental overinvolvement. School personnel do not consider it the parents' responsibility or prerogative to make pedagogical determinations. Parents are viewed as not necessarily possessing the expertise or professional qualifications needed to make such decisions.

Private schools, however, differ from public schools in one important dimension: in their ability to set explicit limits to parental participation in school affairs. Parents must make an explicit choice when selecting a private school. Our case studies reveal that much of their ability to affect the educational experience of their children may be considerably curtailed thereafter. Parents and students may not be as influential in private educational establishments in the way claimed by proponents of educational markets and private education.

Shalom Ieladim was founded in 1990 as a community-based, egalitarian, K to 5 Jewish day school. Although the school draws students from an extensive geographic area, Shalom Ieladim serves primarily the high-income neighborhood where it resides. Most parents are professionals in the service or technology industries. The yearly tuition rate is $7,000. For the school to remain diverse and open to the community, it allocates approximately 20 percent of the operating budget each year to need-based scholarships for those who cannot afford full tuition payments. Over the past few years, the steady increase in the number of applicants to the school's limited openings has prompted the school board to engage in an $11,000,000 fund-raising campaign to double the size of the school. Shalom Ieladim has also received monies from an external donor agency to develop a middle school that will operate in the current school site.

Each classroom has about 24 students and is co-taught by two teachers. Classroom instructors are responsible for imparting the standard general studies program. Specialized teachers are in charge of Judaic studies, Hebrew, physical education, art, and music. This two-tiered curriculum imposes great demands on children, especially in the earlier grades. The full standard general studies program must be crammed into 60 percent of class time. Teachers are permitted and encouraged to emphasize areas of their particular interest—the second-grade teacher focuses on science, while the third-grade teacher focuses on poetry—and a constructivist teaching philosophy permeates the school.

Parents and community members are encouraged to participate in curricular activities. In the lower grades, for instance, students, assigned to different worktables, worked assiduously writing their personal journals with the assistance of parents. Parents are also required to perform 25 hours of school community service or otherwise may elect to serve for a shorter period and pay $25 per unworked hour. Some of the activities that parents provide include office support, photocopying, sending bulk mailings, checking in books at the library, soliciting contributions from prospective donors, or serving on school board subcommittees.

Parents have high expectations of Shalom Ieladim. They have not chosen this school merely because it can provide a Jewish education; they expect it to attain excellence in the general studies program as well. Furthermore, parents have clear opinions of the type of learning that their children should be engaged in. Their view of the school is that of a service provider that ought to cater to the individual needs of their children. The principal describes the relationship between parents and the school in this manner: "It's an entitlement situation here. Parents feel—I think because they're paying money—more empowered to tell you every specific thing, every issue that they have, as if the child was in home schooling away from home." Teachers largely concur with this characterization:

> There's pressure from the parents about what they think should be taught in classes and it may not always be based on an educational framework of knowledge. And they don't always have the information they need to know what is the best thing. Because they're paying for the school sometimes they

feel [that] . . . this is a community school and they want the chance to be involved. But they sometimes think that this means they are the ones that should decide what needs to be done.

Parental voice does indeed carry a significant weight in school matters. After all, the board that makes all school policy determinations is composed largely of parents. Last year, parents on the school board, supported by other parents and the principal, successfully insisted that the school become accredited, requiring the introduction of standardized testing. Shalom Ieladim's teachers are unhappy about this development. They are concerned that it will change the curricular focus of the school, because students will be appraised on standardized tests, rather than on portfolios and more qualitative measures, and their performance will be compared to that of students in the area's public schools. Parents, however, believe it is important to adopt standard parameters that can legitimate their school as a center of high educational quality, comparable to their community's highly regarded public schools.

Yet Shalom Ieladim has also drawn specific boundaries with regard to parental involvement. Primarily, pedagogical decisions are the prerogative of the school's professional staff. The principal fosters open discussion between parents and teachers on matters regarding the learning of their children, but he attempts to assuage those that express an "ongoing overly concerned" attitude. One of his roles within the school is to fend off the "meddling" of parents in daily curricular matters. As a board member declares, "the school does not exist to serve parents. The school exists to deliver excellent education to families and it takes more than the parents' view to accomplish that." While Shalom Ieladim welcomes parent participation in classrooms, parents are not welcomed to decide what will be taught or how. In the words of the school principal, "The position of this school is that parents and the school are not on equal footing. [Shalom Ieladim] has a right to set its own rules and guidelines. The school is open to input from parents, but it is not a cooperative. There is no shared decision making. Parents put in their money and have a say in what goes on, but the ultimate decision is that of the school."

By preventing parents from imposing pedagogical or curricular determinations in classroom practices and defending the professional judgment of teachers, the principal upholds the responsibility of teachers and that of the school as a whole over educational outcomes. The general philosophy embraced is that the obligation of parents is to backstop the efforts of the school, not to fulfill its mission.

Parents at Liniers French School face even stricter boundaries in their ability to influence school affairs than parents at Shalom Ieladim. This private elementary school serves French-national and American bilingual families of highly educated engineers, scientists, and other professionals. French is the primary medium of instruction, and English constitutes less than a quarter of the weekly instruction. Its academic program not only is preparatory for American secondary schools, but is also accredited by the French government to deliver the standard French elementary school curriculum. The administration deliberately attempts to recruit as many applicants for its limited number of seats as possible. The advantage of this selection process is the ability to choose families who are committed to the school's goals so that the school is not required to constantly exert efforts to create buy-in for the school's vision. Liniers uses a rigorous screening process to ensure that students and their families understand the characteristics of this school's practices, curriculum, and standards before they enroll.

The school's recruitment strategy specifically aims at parents who are willing to accept the curriculum as it stands. Despite this clarity in vision, Liniers faces a variety of challenges to keep its clientele satisfied. On one hand, parents of children who will eventually attend secondary school in France consider English lessons as detracting from preparation for French secondary school admission exams. On the other hand, parents of American children perceive time spent in English classes as insufficient. To address these conflicting demands, the school administration and teachers have frequent contact with parents to discuss the value of the compromises made to pursue two distinct curricula simultaneously. But where these tensions persist, the school frequently advises parents that Liniers may not be the school for them. "Sometimes parents are really concerned that the level of English is not going to be exactly the same as in an American school. Of course, because the time spent in English classes is going to be less. So if this is a big concern for parents, my idea would be that our school may be not exactly the school they are looking for . . . because our school is not for everybody."

In other words, Liniers lays out quite clearly that it does not intend to bend to parent wishes. This results in a self-selected group of parents who embrace wholeheartedly the school's bilingual immersion program. A skeptical teacher notes that, in spite of Liniers' open and communicative culture, "people who don't fit into the school get weeded out."

Parents are active members of this school community. Teachers and administrators alike remark on the extensive involvement of parents in various roles such as fund raising, chaperoning, and planning trips, so much so that "they make the school work." A strong and functioning parent–teacher association (PTA) provides the formal structure for this collaborative relationship. In addition, the school plays the role of a congregation point or community center for some parents and a support system for the French families who are new to the area. This informal atmosphere of camaraderie among parents, teachers, and administrators is considered one of the school's assets and, through informal social interaction, contributes to a strong relationship between parents and teachers.

But reflecting on the nature of a desirable parent–teacher partnership, teachers emphasize the importance of parental participation in a "complementary" role rather than a directive one. For instance, one teacher indicates that he expects parents to make appointments with him, rather than dropping by the classroom unannounced. Furthermore, teachers have explicit expectations from parents with regard to how they should support the school's academic program. Parents are required to spend substantial time each day with their children on homework to guarantee that the schools' ambitious academic goals are covered. In the lower grades, parents are also expected to volunteer frequently to support instruction. It might be said that Liniers has partially turned the table around. The school is accountable to parents for delivering student achievement on its own terms, with little interference from parents in the approach that it espouses, while also holding parents accountable to the school for doing their share to advance their children's learning.

PARENTAL INVOLVEMENT IN UPPER-INCOME PUBLIC SCHOOLS

"Why should I listen to you when you can't even put a comma in the right place?"

The desire of high-income parents to engage in and steer pedagogical practices is also a common feature of public schools. Tatuna Point Elementary School sits in a high-income suburb whose affluent families demand the very best public education for their children. Tatuna Point was named a State Distinguished School based on its outstanding schoolwide program. Academic expectations are high across the board, and student achievement is taken extremely seriously by school staff, parents, and students alike. School scores in the Iowa Tests of Basic Skills (ITBS) rank Tatuna Point between the 92 and the 99 national percentiles in reading, language, and mathematics for grades 2 through 5.

Parental involvement, both financially and in time, is a salient characteristic of this school community. On any given day, parents can be found working in the classrooms, shelving books in the Guided Learning Center, manning the computer lab, and directing a variety of sports, art, and music programs. Most classrooms, and especially those in the lower grades, benefit from daily parental help for working in small groups for reading and math, correcting spelling tests, or assisting teachers in a variety of other ways. In recent months, parents have also assumed responsibility for some clerical duties.

Parents do not take their children's education lightly at Tatuna Point. They are a devoted and organized group that make their expectations and demands clear to the staff and administration. In the words of one parent:

> Parents here are willing to be very vocal and express their concerns, or shall we say "whine." Most of the parents, because they're highly educated, put a real premium on education and therefore expect a lot from the schools. They expect high performance and make a lot of demands on the staff, on the principal, on the curriculum. But on the other hand, the majority of those parents say, "I want this, but what can I do to help you get it?" It's not just "I want you to do this, this, and this." My take is that they're willing to back up their demands, if you will, with support, either financial or hands-on. It's a really involved school.

The school principal agrees with this characterization:

> The thing that stands out first, if you look at the general picture of this school, is the parent involvement. That isn't to say that I would rank it at a higher level than the actual teaching going on, but one of the things that really makes the school unique is the incredible parent participation on a continual daily, night, weekend basis. Last year the PTA counted over 8,000 hours of volunteer time here, and that doesn't count anyone who forgot to sign in or was involved and somehow no one knew it.

Parents at Tatuna Point can exert a great deal of influence in school decisions. They can affect what happens in the classroom through two different means: (1) by providing resources to the school and determining how these resources are to be used, and (2) by raising their concerns with the appropriate authorities and demanding observance of their exhortations. And when parents talk, the school must listen attentively.

The three principal avenues for parental volunteerism are the Parent Teacher Association (PTA), the Tatuna Point Educational Foundation (TPEF), and the School Site Council.

PTA members are responsible for organizing and managing a large number of the additional enrichment opportunities supported at Tatuna Point, such as band, gifted and talented education classes, and French and Glee clubs. The PTA also donates $50,000 yearly in capital goods such as playground and computer equipment. An ombudsman team made up of parent volunteers researches and answers fellow parent issues regarding school administration for publication in the school's weekly bulletin.

In 1991, a group of committed parents founded TPEF, a nonprofit foundation, to raise funds to provide additional resources for the improvement of the quality of education of local children. TPEF's focus to date has been improving the staff–student ratio through the funding of additional teachers, consultants, and classroom aides.

The School Site Council includes the principal, teachers, other staff, and parents. Its objective is to serve as a "vehicle by which the school community would come together to chart the school's path to improvement." Some of its main responsibilities include the allocation of available supplemental funds and school-based funds, the development and review of the school plan, including the budget, and the assessment and coordination of the school plan with district goals and efforts.

Parents pour a substantial amount of resources into the school to support its educational mission. Participation in school affairs through volunteerism, in-kind donations, or funding of staff positions augments their visibility and entitles them to a stronger voice within the educational system. Classroom aides sponsored through the Tatuna Point Educational Foundation, for example, are not only accountable to teachers and the school administration for their work, but they are closely monitored by TPEF's board of governors to warrant that the foundation's objectives are being met. An evaluation of resource teachers and classroom aides was conducted by TPEF, the Site School Council, and some independent parents to appraise whether students received more individualized attention. Teachers were requested to keep a log of aides' time every day for one week, and classrooms were formally observed by a team of parents. Formal assessments were written and brought up with the school administration at a School Site Council. This report reckoned that "in the primary grades, 77% of aide time was spent working with small groups or individual students and 23% was spent in clerical duties. In the upper grades, 38% of aide time was spent in working with small groups or individual students and 62% was spent in clerical duties." In the latter case, this was found to be unacceptable and the principal was requested to discuss with upper-grade teachers the "appropriate use" of classroom aides.

The principal describes Tatuna Point's community as people who "know what they want. Many work in entrepreneurial or high-level industry positions where they're used to getting what they want when they want it. And they can come in and be quite demanding." Parents are confident about what they believe is best for their children's education. Furthermore, they often do not trust the educational system to deliver it. A classroom instructor characterizes parental attitudes toward teachers in these words: "Why should I listen to you when you can't even put a comma in the right place?", alluding to parents' self-assurance extending to correction of a teacher's punctuation.

Parents have a clear view about what they deem ought to be happening in the classroom and have little qualms in letting teachers know what their expectations are in terms of instructional practice. They will exert their influence in the classroom, in the principal's office, and at the district level to ensure that their children benefit from a high-quality education that is specifically tailored to their particular needs. Classes are conscientiously monitored, and if a deficiency is perceived, it is immediately addressed and a remedial course of action demanded.

Teachers appreciate and welcome the cooperation of parents in class and value the additional resources that they bring into the classroom. An instructor, for example, commented that "I've been at schools that didn't have any parental support and it makes a huge difference to have parent support and I think that helps to make a good school." Resentment, on the other hand, arises when parents question the professional competence of teachers and attempt to make determinations about what ought to be taking place in the classroom and how. "I'm heavily influenced by the parents only because my parent communication is very heavy. I write to them every week and they write back to me every week on every single student I deal with. What they say to me—I don't take it personally. I know that professionally I'm doing the right thing. If they're doubting my professionalism or what I'm teaching, I'll go over it with them."

Without doubt, teachers at Tatuna Point feel directly accountable to parents, perhaps even more so than to the school administration or to the district. There is little discussion about formal teacher evaluations with the principal or concern about fulfilling district mandates. The greatest source of worry on a day-to-day basis is beyond doubt parental satisfaction. The issues at stake may include, for example, the amount of homework and its degree of difficulty (or actually lack thereof), curricular design, or pedagogical practice. A teacher uses the controversy surrounding the role of parent-funded teacher aides to illustrate this point: "[Parents] pay for our instructional aides. And it's been an issue how the upper-grade teachers use their aides, because we mostly use them for more clerical type of stuff, not working with students and so forth. It's been brought to our attention. . . . It seems like [parents] want to dictate what happens: 'We're not going to fund it unless you're doing it our way.' "

The work of the principal is not free from the scrutiny of the vigilant eye of Tatuna Point's parents either. As the principal remarks, "Oh, [parents] call the district office if they're not happy. The school district is generally very responsive to parents. If a parent is unhappy about something I do or something that's done via me that the district has done, this community will go to school board meetings. On the class size reduction they've gone. I'm proud of them, because I think if you're going to whine you'd better be prepared to do something."

Parents equate the principal's role in the school to that of "the CEO of [a] business"; and, as a CEO, parents expect the principal to be fully in control of the management, operation, and productivity of her enterprise. Furthermore, they also consider it a priority that she report in full to her "shareholders"—to whom she is accountable—about the health of the "business."

Parents complain "there is not enough communication by the school." These repeated expressions for greater details on the current status and administration of the school, however, seem to have gone haywire. Tatuna Point prints a weekly bulletin that carefully outlines its latest activities and also responds to parent inquiries. The principal must fulfill regular reporting obligations with the three governing bodies of the parent-led organizations. The three parental boards later publish their own individual accounts, which receive mass distribution. In addition, the district puts out an accountability report on the school for the consumption of the community that it services.

Parents wield a lot of influence at Tatuna Point. They comprise a strong accountability system both formally and informally. Not only do they articulate their demands loudly, but they also take the necessary steps to see that their demands are met either by voicing their discontent with teachers, administrators, and district officials directly or by organizing and participating in formal institutions that control and regiment school activities closely. Many teachers find parental pressure to be so stressful that they remain only a brief time at Tatuna Point before requesting transfers to other district schools. Of the school's twenty-four teachers, only five have more than 4 years' tenure at Tatuna Point, a school that, to most outside observers, would seem a desirable place to teach because of its high test scores, affluent student body, and supplementary parent-donated resources.

Like Tatuna Point, Olympic Charter School also benefits from legions of parent volunteers who assist in classrooms, teach units in their specialties, and take responsibility for office administrative duties. Olympic distinguishes itself by its "constructivist" pedagogical philosophy, defined by one teacher as "an environment where children can create or construct their own learning . . . with hands-on activities." With roots in Deweyan progressivism and in the "free" or "open school" movement of the 1960–70s, the school selects teachers as well as parents select the school based on their adherence to this philosophy. Although physically located in a lower-middle class community, the school's Constructivist philosophy tends to appeal disproportionately (though not exclusively) to upper-middle class professional families.[4]

Yet, in spite of this explicit self-identification, which all parents understand before selecting the school, teachers report that their greatest challenge is to defend the school's pedagogical orientation. An instructor reports that, on her first day of teaching, twenty-five parents visited her classroom with specific suggestions about how the curriculum ought to be organized. Overall, parents demand a greater emphasis on basic skills. These demands reflect the expectation that a greater focus on basic skills will gain their children higher scores on standardized tests. One teacher, for instance, recounted that she had increased the importance of memorization of multiplication tables in her curriculum in order to "pacify the parents." When not willing to abdicate, teachers must be willing to channel their energies into resisting parental pressures. An instructor described a year-long dispute with a parent about the teacher's tolerance of spelling errors in a second-grader's creative writing. The teacher finally told the parent, "you can correct your child's spelling at home, but we're not going to do it."

From the perspective of Olympic Charter's faculty and parent leaders, conflict with parents who cannot accept the school's off-beat style is resolved, ideally, not when the school accommodates itself to parental demands, but rather when the school has communicated its philosophy so unequivocally that parents withdraw their children once they become convinced that the school will not meet their objectives. But while some parents withdraw if the school does not meet their needs, most others attempt to change it. Two years ago, there were so many parent complaints about curricular matters that the teachers rebelled and, as a result, Olympic's governing structure was revised: the charter's parent majority on the governing board was replaced with a teacher majority. According to the principal, "teachers want to maintain the stance that the curriculum really is theirs. Ownership. They own the curriculum, and they don't want the parents to have the feeling that they can interfere."

A similar pattern in the nature of the relationship between educators and parents could be observed at Adams Charter Middle School, a small-town public charter school. Adams Charter enrolls only seventy-five seventh- and eighth-grade students. Like Olympic Charter, it is under the direct jurisdiction of the local school district and receives most of its financing from public funds. Yet, in some respects, Adams Charter functions more like a private than a public school. It does not accept bilingual or special education students and it screens other applicants for academic fit before acceptance. While there is no formal tuition, there is a minimum monthly "pledge" of $85 and other mandatory requirements for parent participation and fund raising. At Adams, children cannot enroll unless their parents commit to 8 hours of volunteer service in the school per month, a requirement that they can also fulfill by substituting an additional financial contribution or by purchasing "scrip" in excess of the monthly requirement of $200.[5]

Adams Charter parents participate actively in school activities in fulfillment of their volunteer requirements. There are almost always parents assisting in classrooms and performing other duties, such as running the physical education program for which no teacher is assigned. The presence of parents in educational matters gives Adams a distinctive character. But parental overinvolvement in the academic matters, however, is also now beginning to be perceived by the faculty as an important concern.

Adams Charter was founded by parents who had previously home schooled their children. The parents and founding teachers sought charter status because they could access public funds to design a school with a distinctive curricular model focused on the arts. The school building is a converted arts gallery, and student artwork is displayed throughout. An artist was a school founder (he remains a teacher at the school), and the school attempts to use the arts to integrate the entire curriculum, "not just the art for the art's sake, but the creative thinking that happens when you get to know art and be involved in art and creativity."

Yet, despite the curricular vision of the founders, parents recently pressured the staff to add algebra to the eighth-grade curriculum over the objections of teachers. As a board member in the parent-led governing body recounts, "we did not have an algebra class in place, and if it had been left up to the principal and the teachers, or specifically the math teachers, we probably wouldn't have had an algebra class. But there was a group of us who felt very strongly about offering algebra, and we pushed it through. And so, we have algebra."

Like the principals at Olympic Charter and Tatuna Point, the principal of Adams Charter now worries that this level of parental interference will become a more common phenomenon and that parents will start "second guessing every aspect of the curriculum." If parents become this involved, the principal says, the school "will have chaos."

These examples suggest that parents of public school pupils, when they act collectively, can be a powerful pressure group that evaluates as well as influences classroom curricular policies, pedagogical approaches, or the handling of children's socioemotional development. If dissatisfied with the school's response, parents often turn to district officials or to elected school board members to air their concerns. As many educators attest, their voices can ring loudly.

TRENDS IN CLIENT ORIENTATION IN PRIVATE VERSUS PUBLIC SCHOOLS

Overall, our observations suggest a pattern in which higher-income parents tend to be more involved than lower-income parents in a variety of school activities. They are also more at ease in challenging schools with regard to educational practices. Parental demands for accountability and their disposition toward academic involvement vary more by social class than by whether a school is public or private. Although similar opportunities for participation are present in most educational settings, less educated parents tend to participate much less in their children's schools, public or private. Socioeconomic factors help to explain this difference.

In lower-income schools, whether Mashita Middle School or St. Donat's Catholic School, most working parents cannot fulfill volunteer classroom assignments during the regular school day. Less educated parents are more likely to have younger children at home, to both work full time, or to be impeded from freely communicating with school staff by limited English-language proficiency. Even if they could come to school, few feel that they have the academic skills necessary to assist in a significant way in an educational program. They tend to perceive teachers and administrators as professionals of a higher social standing and do not feel qualified to evaluate or challenge their practices.

One school in our sample was an exception to this general principle. United Primary, a public school, was more successful than others in organizing parental involvement in the educational program, but its success seems to be rooted in its nonacademic activities. United acted as a community service center, developing parental commitment to the school by delivering a range of health, social, and educational services. The school favored a whole-family approach, making great efforts to integrate the curriculum with its community and encouraging parents to communicate with the school by hiring multilingual staff. Renaissance Middle School has also recently espoused a similar school policy, providing parents with a range of social services within the school. There was initial indication that this approach was starting to pay off. English as a second language classes, for example, brought a number of Asian parents to a school that they previously feared because of communication barriers and a reputation of violence. A Family Literacy Night brought three hundred parents in to see their children's work displayed and to recognize student achievements. This comprehensive approach to schooling goes beyond the efforts we saw at most other low-income schools, public or private. Certainly, it will not be easy for other schools to espouse this model of educational change. The coordination of a range of social and educational services is an expensive endeavor. Such coordination, however, is becoming more common in low-income community public schools.

Teachers and administrators believe that parental disengagement is highly detrimental to student achievement; hence, they attempt to stimulate parental participation in a variety of ways. Lower-income parents tend to be less vocal and participate less. They are usually "invited" into the school to participate and their role is often limited to supporting school directives. Many private and charter schools have made parental volunteerism a condition for admission. Under present laws, this option is not viable for neighborhood public schools, regardless of how much the faculty wishes it were otherwise. Nor is it apparent, even if such a condition could be legally imposed, how it could be enforced.[6]

The concept of parental involvement, however, bears an important distinction to parental accountability. In lower-income schools, both public and private, parents are urged to assume greater responsibility for children's academic and behavioral outcomes. In private and charter schools, this type of involvement is usually mandatory. In either case, however, the terms of parental participation are largely defined and determined by school professionals. This kind of participation is akin to making parents accountable to the schools, rather than the other way around.

In public and private schools from high-income settings, parents comprise a vocal group that make explicit their expectations for an education of the highest quality for their children. They exercise little reservation in expressing clearly their views, concerns, and demands to school administrators and teachers. They feel entitled to making judgments about the quality of education provision that their children receive and demand that deficiencies be redressed. They also show little hesitation in turning to the highest possible authorities to make their opinions known. They not only expect to be listened to, but they also expect that their exhortations will lead to concrete action toward the fulfillment of their wishes.

Yet our case studies highlight an important difference between the private and the public sector. As private institutions, private schools demonstrate a greater capacity to shield teachers and administrators from parental demands. As illustrated by the educators at Shalom Ieladim or Liniers, there is a conviction that school decisions are school prerogatives. It is not the place of parents to set educational policy. Their obligation is to support the school's mission, not steer it. They do not have ownership—hence, a mandate to make school determinations. Parents are primarily consumers of the services that their school furnishes.

Private schools, overall, have proved to be quite successful in establishing clear boundaries for parental involvement in school internal affairs. This general trend can be detected in lower-income private schools, just as it was observable among their higher-income counterparts. Knuckleborough School, for instance, is a private for-profit school in a predominantly lower middle income neighborhood. It is housed in a three-building complex, just two blocks from one of the city's central thoroughfares. The main school complex has been converted from a grocery store to house classrooms and administrative offices. There is a single-story building that is subdivided by partition walls into classrooms and the school library. A two-room semipermanent structure houses classrooms and a cement playground. A few trees and plants are growing in brightly painted planter boxes that have been placed around the fenced-in playground. There are no cafeteria, auditorium, gym, or playing fields. Administrators, parents, and teachers describe the school's facilities as everything from "unconventional," "unorthodox," and "funky" to "unattractive," "depressing," and "breeding a certain amount of chaos."

Knuckleborough stands out from the rest of the schools in our sample by the explicitness with which the school's accountability to parents is restricted. The proprietors have maintained a clear policy of discouraging parental involvement to prevent interference in the school's operation. Although the owner maintains that "parents are welcomed here with open arms," their role has been largely circumscribed to school beautification programs in the playground. Any other type of intervention has been actively discouraged. "It's been made very clear to them," attests the owner, "that they may *not* come into the classrooms and decide that they want to change the curriculum. That is *our* responsibility, and they understand it."

Until recently, and for most of the school's 28-year existence, there has been no parent association or other parent advisory group. Parents are not encouraged to assist in classrooms either. The reasons behind the reluctance to allow the formation of a parent group, according to one teacher, are two: "One, [the founder] did not want any parents meddling in the academic program. But, most importantly, he understood that . . . you've got to be in the classroom and you've got to deal with the program of the school. You can't spend an inordinate amount of time working with parents who are very demanding."

It ought to be highlighted that Knuckleborough does not espouse any particular curricular focus. In the lower grades, teachers follow a curriculum set forth in a textbook series, whereas in the upper grades the school provides no curricular guidelines to teachers. Not surprisingly, teachers, particularly those in the upper grades, complain that there is too little curricular direction. Parents, nonetheless, are quite satisfied with Knuckleborough. Most students remain in the school for their entire 9-year elementary school careers. The school's attractiveness can be attributed in part to a unique service that public schools can't match: an eleven-and-a-half-hour day, which includes pre- and afterschool programs designed for working parents.

In the last year, the proprietor gave in to parental pressure and permitted an advisory group to form, but she is reluctant to permit it to become too involved in the school's operations. In part, this slight weakening of the proprietor's resolve is due to growing financial pressures faced by the school and the desire to ask parents to engage in tax-deductible fund raising activities. Yet the school administration remains so fearful of parental involvement that Knuckleborough refuses to distribute class rosters with student home phone numbers, purportedly to protect families' privacy, but in actuality to prevent parents from organizing pressure of any kind against the school. The school's philosophy, the principal underscores, is "leave them at the gate, we'll educate!"

Private schools can shield themselves from parental influence behind their entitlement to follow their own educational mission and vision. Parents' main recourse is exit. Ultimately, families are presented with two choices: to accept the school as it is or to find a different institution that better suits their educational expectations. In other words, parents may have the choice to exit private schooling, but their voice is limited to temper what occurs within schools.

Two Catholic schools that recently disbanded their parent advisory councils because parents became too aggressive in proposing policy changes to the school leadership illustrate the limits of accountability for parents in private schools. At St. Felipe's, a group of parents on the school board became excessively—in the principal's view—critical of a teacher. The response from the principal and the pastor was to disband the advisory board altogether. At St. Barbara's, leaders of the parent council had certain concerns about the direction that the school was taking. They thought that discipline was too lax at the school, that pedagogies to impart basic skills (like phonics) were insufficiently emphasized in instruction, and that the school did not assign enough homework. After much argument with parents, the principal in conjunction with the school pastor broke up the council and communicated to parents that they were free to take their children elsewhere if they did not approve of how the school was run.

In turn, the claims of private market supporters notwithstanding, parents in public schools can command at least as much as or perhaps even more control over educational issues than parents in private. On careful reflection, this makes sense. Public education is a public service, in principle serving the public good. Parents should be able to influence what goes on in the public school. Society has an interest in the kind of education that its children receive, and this should be an arena for debate.

Parents of children in public school may have limited opportunities for exit; sometimes the only alternative is having the means to afford a private education. And parental interests may in fact compete with numerous demands from other school and district sources. But our case studies evidence that parents, like those at Tatuna Point, can and often do constitute a powerful pressure group that can set change in motion. Furthermore, parents may not only exercise their voice at the school level, but they also have a say at the district and state level through the ballot box.

Charter schools walk a fine line between the approaches espoused by the public and private sector. Their administrators and faculty, such as those at Olympic and Adams, may attempt to discourage the enrollment of children whose parents do not subscribe to the school's self-defined mission. But this process must be subtle, because the law does not permit public charters to exclude children on philosophical grounds. This is a feature of private education, where schools offer a self-defined product and parents either accept it or withdraw.

In addition, charter schools, just as private schools have, may also increasingly mandate parental participation to support their children's academic progress. As a condition for enrollment, schools may require parents to make a commitment to read to their children every evening or assist with their children's homework. Charter and private schools, such as St. Barbara's or Madison Charter, are increasingly making explicit demands to parents and attempt to hold them to some extent accountable for their children's academic progress.

Charter schools have also shown some resilience in mediating or resisting perceived parental overinvolvement. At Olympic Charter, for instance, parents are requested to fill out a client satisfaction survey. The receipt of the returned questionnaires is the occasion for a weekend retreat during which the faculty considers what changes might be suggested by the parents' responses. In several cases, teachers reported that they made changes in curricular emphasis based on this feedback. On the other hand, teachers have rebelled at the practice of anonymous parental evaluations, a reflection of their developing frustration about what they regarded as excessive parental interference. Furthermore, in the face of extensive calls for shifts in the curriculum from parents, teachers were able to convince the governing board of Olympic Charter to change the charter's parent majority and replace it with a greater number of seats allocated to educators.

This example stands in stark contrast to Tatuna Point, where parents feel they have a right to shape and influence their community school and where the school feels an obligation to address and respond to parental demands. Public schools have a legal mandate to respond to their local constituency. Families may choose to exit to the private school system, but they may also exercise their ability to try to change what goes on in their schools.

Because the model of parent–consumer sovereignty is often held up as an ideal for educational reform, our case studies offer policy makers and educators a distinct reality check. In the first place, the empirical evidence does not confirm that the private sector may be necessarily more responsive or accountable to parental demands. No school was more accountable to families for outcomes and pedagogical practices than Tatuna Point Elementary, a public school. Parents of public school children can command as much as or more control over educational issues as do parents of private school children—when the parents are affluent, self-confident, and highly educated. On the other hand, it is private schools, such as Liniers or Knuckleborough, that have sought to discourage parents most overtly from voicing their opinions or have made it clear that those who strive to bring about school change could be in fact "weeded out."

Perhaps most importantly, our data reveal the limitations of an education reform vision founded on parental voice and accountability as an engine for change. We found reason to question the conventional view that making schools more accountable to parents is a certain road to school improvement. A coherent vision of the curriculum or better teaching is not necessarily an automatic outcome of external parental pressures. The faculties of these public and private schools spend much of their time and energy resisting efforts by parents to hold them accountable for—to "meddle" in, the faculties would say—professional decision making in which parents, no matter how well educated, may have a limited perspective. The appropriateness or effectiveness of parent-led initiatives is not a guarantee of educational excellence. Schools and districts still need to develop means to make parental participation useful.

WHAT DO PARENTS LOOK FOR IN A SCHOOL?

Educational models based on consumer sovereignty deem that learning in market-driven private schools is delivered more efficiently than in public schools. This efficiency is oftentimes described as a stronger orientation toward incentive systems that focus on student achievement, rather than on bureaucratic aims, because this is what parents expect. In other words, since private schools depend on customer satisfaction for their survival, they must align themselves with consumer demands for higher achievement in order to endure. Once again, the interviews and observations that we conducted in private and public schools challenge these assumptions.

Our data suggest that schools can organize around a variety of principles, such as academic outcomes, religious beliefs, safety, and discipline. Yet there is no clear demarcation between the private and public sector in terms of the rallying principles around which schools choose to align themselves. In most cases, a variety of principles comes into play. And in most cases, school actors—principals, teachers, parents—do not necessarily agree with each other about how these objectives should be prioritized. This lack of agreement may result in confusion about whether the schools' primary goal is deepening religious faith, transmitting academic skills, or developing disciplined and moral life habits.

An overall trend stands out nonetheless. In low-income private schools, academic goals face greater competition from other school goals, most prominently religious objectives, than in the public sector. However, the challenges that both public and private schools face to foster academic progress are great, because these schools serve children from disadvantaged environments and frequently enjoy limited parental support. Yet, in many private religious schools, educators admit that their challenges are compounded because, in addition to scholastic achievement, they must also attend to, and even give priority to, other instructional aspirations. In higher-income environments, the competition between academic and other goals is also observed, but school administrators and parents alike place great weight on ensuring that their students reach academic excellence standards.

Not unexpectedly, religious objectives are a central and defining mission of parochial and other religious schools. St. Felipe's is a case in point. The parent–student handbook avows that "as a Faith Community, the primary purpose of St. Felipe's School is to lead our students to know, to love, to experience Jesus Christ and to spread His saving message throughout the world." The handbook lists the objectives of the school as being, first, religious; next, moral; next, academic; and, finally, physical, social, and cultural. The handbook goes on to list parent responsibilities in the following order: (1) to "support the teaching of Catholic doctrine, values, traditions and liturgical practices"; (2) to "support the life of the Church through involvement in the . . . parish"; (3) to support the policies of the school, followed by meeting financial obligations and participating in parent meetings. It is only in the seventh and eighth place in this list of goals that academic objectives take center stage. "As partners in education, support the learning process by establishing a regular time for homework, monitoring television viewing and assuring that children receive proper rest, exercise and nutrition." The last goal is to "be well informed regarding academic progress."

St. Milton's handbook shares many similarities with St. Felipe's. It begins by stating that the "distinctive purpose of St. Milton's Catholic School is to proclaim the gospel message of Jesus Christ" and then proceeds to enumerate the school's objectives, with strictly academic outcomes far down on the list. Religious instruction is a primordial objective at these parochial schools, and academics are perceived to follow behind. St. Milton's principal, for instance, states that when religion is properly taught academic outcomes will take care of themselves: "The academics flow from that [religious instruction], but our first and foremost reason for being here is the moral education of the children." Asked to describe the mission of the school, St. Felipe's pastor stated that it was to provide "ways in which people can grow their faith, . . . to grow as followers of Christ, . . . to make sure the children have been taught a rich education, that children who want to are helped to grow in the Catholic faith." The school's principal adds that, although many children at the school are Baptists, "if you are non-Catholic and you attend our school, you must take Catholic religion."

In some cases, religious schools struggle to strike a balance between scholastic and religious goals. At St. Barbara's, there was an ongoing dispute between the parish pastor and the school principal about whether the school's mission was primarily pastoral or academic. Because the school had nearly twice the number of applicants as seats, admission choices frequently had to be made between, on the one hand, students who scored low on academic tests but were children of parishioners and, on the other, students from outside the parish whose academic scores were higher. Often the pastor deferred to the principal's wish to create a school with a strong academic reputation; but just as frequently, the principal was pressured to make exceptions in her admissions policy in favor of parish children who tested poorly. Occasionally, applicants rejected on the basis of low test scores were told that they could reapply if, after a year in the local public school, their test scores had improved. The pastor of St. Barbara's insisted that "we're not a successful school if our students get into Harvard but in the process drop the Catholic Church. The principal reason for the school is to hand down the Catholic faith."

The compromises between academic excellence and religious instruction are less perceptible in higher-income schools, where both objectives are pursued with equal zeal. A board member of Shalom Ieladim, for example, recognizes that parents who say "I want my kid to learn how to read Hebrew, I want my kid to read the Bible in the original, I want my kid to celebrate the Sabbath in the school" are given primacy in their admission procedures "because that's really why we raise money so hard for." Yet high academic achievement is a primary concern for educators and families alike. Parents have high academic expectations of Shalom Ieladim. They have not chosen this school merely because it can provide a Jewish education; they expect it to attain excellence in the general studies program as well. Usually, the demands that this environment places on students are great. At Shalom Ieladim, the rigor of the regular academic curriculum is compounded by the pressures of learning Hebrew and dedicating a significant portion of the school day to Jewish studies. The support from parents outside the classroom is essential in order to attain the objectives that this community aspires to.

Teachers in religious schools that serve children from less advantaged backgrounds in low- and middle-income communities sometimes express reservations about the primacy of religious objectives and admit to emphasizing academics more than does the principal. Several instructors at St. Barbara's, for example, objected to time taken from academic pursuits for religious instruction, participation in Mass or other social-religious activities. Similarly, a lay teacher at St. Donat's confesses that there is only one firm regulation that they must abide by: completing a 45-minute religion unit daily; yet, under pressure, she sometimes cuts catechism to emphasize reading or math:

> If I need to cut into some subjects or not do a subject that day because we need to get to other things, I usually end up cutting out religion. I'll feel kind of guilty about it. This is a Catholic school. But then I'll do something at the end of the day, like saying a prayer. We might not have read the religion book today, but we said a prayer. In all fairness, if I had to pick between something like language or math or cutting out religion, I'm going to cut out religion. . . . English and language and math are just so important.

The salience of religious instruction in these communities is often not a primary interest among parents either. Many families complain that too much time is taken away from academics by religious activities. Yet parents are willing to make great concessions to these private schools' defined missions. Most Catholic schools in our sample, for example, make catechism a compulsory subject within their curriculum. Although in some of these schools non-Catholic students may be a large proportion of the student body, parents agree to have their children partake daily in a 45-minute religious course, as well as in many other religious activities, without exception. This may amount to approximately 15 to 20 percent of the total time that students spend in school.

Some parents acknowledged that they were willing to send their children to a religious school in spite of their heavy focus on religious affairs because they believed that a Catholic school provides academic instruction superior to that of their public counterparts. Others had their eyes on preparing their children to compete for admission to regional academic Catholic high schools, and parochial elementary schools were perceived as a gateway. Yet another theme emerged repeatedly from our interviews regarding why parents in low- and middle-income communities were attracted to private religious schools: they believed them to be safer than public schools. Parents were relatively indifferent to their stated goals and expectations, as long as they perceived the school environment to be free of gangs and violence. Desire for exposure to Catholicism was not the motivating factor for a lot of parents in St. Felipe's or St. Milton's, although it was indeed the case for some. These families sent their children there because they believed that the schools were secure or had a reputation for strict discipline. Traditionally disciplined classrooms, student uniforms, and quiet order were thought as less welcoming to violent behavior.

This also proved to be the case at St. Donat's. Safety, not religion, was the reason why many parents have opted for this school. A parent underscores that seeing the school door closed is what she likes best of St. Donat's. "Here you have to ring the bell to get in. Nobody can open the door. The students are good and I like it because I believe all the teachers are looking for security for their children." While some parents thought that St. Donat's offered a superior academic education, a teacher assessed typical parents of her students this way: "They'll agree to the religion even if they don't necessarily want it that much . . . because they want their kid in a safe place." The principal agreed with this characterization:

> I think if you were to ask most parents why they send their children, especially send them to a private school, a Catholic school, it would be safety. Twenty years ago they wouldn't have said this. It's a safe environment. Discipline and maybe religion would sit somewhere down the line. But that's not a top priority. We stress the fact that we're a religious school.

And I think subconsciously it's there. But when you talk to them, "I like my children here because I feel safe with my children in this school. Nothing will happen to them. I trust the people who are taking care of my children during the day." I think that's the number one that I hear. It's not "I'm sending my child to this school because I want to pass the faith on to my children." I don't hear that. I did thirty, forty years ago, but not now.

Overall, the reputation of these private schools rests largely on safety and discipline maintenance. There is little indication that these schools are organized around excellence in academic achievement. Student expectations tend to be low; and teachers feel constrained by the lack of resources as well as by the social and emotional baggage that many of their students bring from home. Private schools, however, bear one advantage over the public sector. They have the prerogative to refuse admission to applicants or to return students with academic and behavioral problems to the public system. When private schools cannot cope, parents are advised to transfer their children to public schools where there are "more resources" and students can receive "better and more appropriate services" to their needs.

The lower-income public schools in our sample face many of the same challenges as their private counterparts: children from disadvantaged backgrounds with behavioral and emotional problems, poor parent support, resource inadequacies, low academic expectations, and weak academic results. But, despite these severe constraints, the discourse, if not the practice, of academic excellence remains quite explicit. The concern over student academic performance and progress seems to have grown increasingly louder in recent years. For example, United Primary School adopted the mission that all children are college bound. "The expectations are pretty high in relationship to other schools that have similar populations," admits the principal. This vision was initially expressed by families, but was then picked up and officially articulated by the principal. Although received with some trepidation from teachers at the beginning, the objective to pursue the highest academic goals won support from the entire school community.

Similarly, Renaissance's philosophy holds as a central tenet that "all individuals can learn." Located in the poorest region of the city and isolated from other neighborhoods by the hills enclosing the valley and a highway that cuts across its base, Renaissance finds itself not far from a housing project that was closed due to high drug and crime rates and generally deplorable conditions. After being reconstituted by the local school district for its inability to improve student academic performance, Rennaissance started all over with a new principal and staff. This was the beginning of a turnaround that grounded the school around academic achievement as an attainable goal for all students. The school mission is summarized in the following eleven principles:

1. All individuals can learn.
2. All individuals are both potential learners and potential teachers.
3. All individuals want to learn and to be recognized for their achievements.
4. All individuals are entitled to be treated with respect and dignity.
5. Learning can be subdivided into a number of specific, concrete competencies that can be used as a focus for teaching.
6. All individuals should learn to live and work in a world that is characterized by interdependence and cultural diversity.
7. Learning has both cognitive and affective dimensions.
8. If individuals do not learn, then those assigned to be their teachers should accept responsibility for this failure and should take appropriate remedial action.
9. All individuals learn in many different ways and at varying rates.

10. Each individual learns best in a particular way.
11. Parents want their children to attain their fullest potential as learners and to succeed academically.

Ayacucho Elementary has also undergone a similar shift, from academic indifference to a much greater scholastic focus. In this case, this process began without much prompting from the local district or its recent immigrant Latino parents. Ayacucho was in fact one of the first schools in the district where a principal sought to change the educational vision of a school. A number of reforms were implemented to advance student learning and academic achievement. For example, traditional teaching methods were replaced by a child-centered, developmental approach. Phonics-based instruction was abandoned for whole-language instruction instead. With professional support, teachers received training on cooperative learning, setting standards and expectations and implementing a hands-on curriculum. Students were assigned to multiage classrooms, and student evaluation was moved from letter-graded to narrative report cards.

Yet, despite this effort to focus on academic success as their primary responsibility, public schools in economically disadvantaged areas, like their private sector counterparts, are most likely to be held accountable by parents for nonacademic outcomes. Parents will voice alarm and hold schools responsible for their children's behavior or safety. At Ayacucho, for instance, parents remain largely uninvolved in academics, but out of concern about the potential danger of students running into a nearby highway, they successfully demanded that the school build a fence. Parents also mobilize to protect the standing or behavior of their own children. As teachers told us at St. Milton's, St. Donat's, and Mashita, parents not only refuse to take blame for their children's misconduct, but they are quick to reproach teachers for their inability to keep them under control. The following anecdote from an assistant principal at

Renaissance serves as a telling story to illustrate the tensions between the expectations of parents and educators with regard to the role of schools, academic achievement, and student behavior.

> If there is a discipline issue and I have to send [a] kid home or something, and I call and ask for a parent conference, they may be mad and they'll curse me out. I let them vent and then I say, "Remember, I want what you want for your child."
>
> For example, one lady called and said, "Ms. Jones, I'm coming up there" and, I quote, "to kick your ass! You're calling me and asking me to come. Well, I don't know what to do with this child, and you should know something to do, and since you don't, that's what I'm gonna do." And she said, "Do I still have to come?" and I said, "Yes, you still have to come. You still have to come if you want the child to come back to school and you still have to have a parent conference with me." So she said, "I'll be up there and I will kick your ass and I mean it." Bam! She slammed the phone down.
>
> The next morning I was expecting her. She came up and I talked to her outside but she didn't want to speak. I invited her to come in [to my office]. She was really mad. She just sat there. So I said, "William, tell your mother what Ms. Jones wants for you and what this school wants for you." And William said, "You want me to graduate from Renaissance, and you want me to graduate from high school." And when she heard that, that woman just broke out in tears. She cried and said, "Ms. Jones, I am so sorry. I am so sorry I cursed you out." I said, "Why do you have all these tears?" She said, "I never realized he could graduate from high school." I said, "See, we want the best for him too."

The efforts channeled into enhancing academic performance in public schools have not necessarily had clear payoffs. At Ayacucho, although the child-centered pedagogies embraced had the best interests of students in mind and sought to improve students' reading skills, they had little effect on student achievement. Even with ongoing efforts by teachers and the school administration, students' test scores continue to be the lowest in the district. In fact, in the most recent language arts assessment using the district standard, 81 percent of first graders, 69 percent of second graders, 67 percent of third graders, and 55 percent of fourth graders in the school did not pass. Raising students' reading scores remains the primary focus of the school, but so does the question of how best to achieve these results.

United and Renaissance's explicit focus on high academic achievement is supported through a comprehensive set of community outreach, family health, and social work services. While these programs may have value in themselves, it remains to be seen whether, or to what extent, they will succeed in their academic objectives. These schools' emphasis on social programs may turn out to conflict with the clarity of their academic ambitions. Renaissance teachers find the school's lofty academic expectations to be inconsistent with the disadvantages that their students face, leading many to leave in frustration. Teachers at United have also expressed some skepticism about how to turn high academic expectations into a reality. It is unclear whether United's goal that every student will be college bound can be realized without defined intermediate benchmarks than can serve as a practical guide for educators. In the shorter term, teachers at both Renaissance and United were unhappy about their district's emphasis on standardized testing, which they viewed as forcing them to emphasize narrow testable skills to the exclusion of other equally important academic goals.

In summary, parents from lower-income schools, both public and private, appeared to be less inclined to give primacy to academic objectives. Nonacademic matters, such as school safety and behavioral concerns, took precedence over strict academic concerns. From the perspective of school principals and administrators, leaders in lower-income private religious schools made explicit the prominence of their religious purpose. Spiritual goals were undoubtedly at the core of the mission and organizational structure of these schools. These goals, however, were not always completely shared by the school staff. The discourse in lower-income public schools, in turn, seemed more focused around academic expectations and pedagogical matters. Questions such as how realistic high academic expectations in socioeconomically disadvantaged environments are or what the most effective educational paths to attain these goals might be were the source of a lively debate among school staff. The challenge in the low-income public sector schools remains to translate this vision into reality.

There were no significant differences in middle- to higher-income schools in the public and private sectors with regard to the primacy they gave to academic objectives. Both types of schools organize themselves around clear scholastic goals, driven with equal ardor by school administrators, teachers, and parents. Often the debate centered around parents who wanted to see their children perform well in standardized tests and teachers who strove to defend constructivist pedagogies and a broader approach to general education. Compared to their counterparts in public schools, students in higher-income religious schools face significant demands from ambitious curricular programs that embrace both academic and spiritual objectives with equal zest. Teachers and school administrators rely on the support and dedication of parents and students to accomplish successfully these multiple goals.

SOME CONCLUSIONS

Many analysts have claimed that private schools are more willing and able than public schools to respond to parents and to organize themselves around high academic achievement. In our study of sixteen schools, we found no evidence of such systematic differences. True, our study was of primary elementary and middle schools, and most of these claims are based on secondary school data. But at least at the lower levels of schooling, the notion that parental choice and private management of schools make educational establishments more responsive to families and raise schools' focus and efficiency in delivering academic achievement does not necessarily hold. Neither does the notion that the organization of public schools governed under bureaucratic norms is dominated by numerous interest groups, resulting in dissatisfied teachers, frustrated parents, and a weaker academic orientation.

The trends discernible from our case studies do not relate to differences between private and public sector schools. Rather, there is a striking resemblance between higher-income schools, both public and private. Similarly, there is a striking resemblance between lower-income schools, both public and private. In the former case, high-income parents comprise a vocal group. They have strong opinions and they do not hesitate to make their voice heard with teachers, principals, and school authorities. When parents speak, school administrators and educators listen. Academic achievement is a high priority, and parents are able to mobilize extensive financial and human resources to support schools in the pursuit of their children's scholastic success. Public schools with students from higher-income families are just as likely to be accountable to their parents for academic outcomes as are private schools serving the same clientele.

Lower-income parents tend to demonstrate limited involvement in their children's education. Teachers and principals dedicate significant efforts to garner and secure their support, often, but not always, with limited results. Furthermore, parents in lower-income private and public schools do not necessarily prioritize academic achievement. Their focus tends to be directed toward nonacademic goals, such as safety and discipline.

With regard to their alignment with academic objectives, in higher-income schools the entire school community rallies behind the attainment of scholastic excellence. The debates on which pedagogical approaches—whether a focus on child-centered constructivist learning, basic skills drills, or progress on testable outcomes—may be most effective to maximize academic achievement are lively, and sometimes they may even turn thorny, but these discussions among school administrators, teachers, and parents represent a stalwart belief in the pursuit of academic knowledge as a key role of schooling. This is so in the private as well as the public domain. In lower-income schools, on the other hand, the challenges of serving a student population that is socioeconomically disadvantaged frequently raise some doubts among school actors about the possibility of fulfilling high academic expectations. Schools, public and private alike, must engage in a balancing act in which the promotion of academic progress is conditioned by other social and psychoemotional demands.

Private schools, operating in markets, have the prerogative to offer educational packages that vary considerably from typical public education. In some cases, private schools may focus their services around academic programs that promote a particular method of teaching (such as a constructivist approach) or embrace an alternative educational product (such as dual-language immersion). These educational packages, however, are not standard features of private establishments. And similar types of programs are found in the public sector. For many if not most private schools, then, we observe that economist Brown (1992) was mostly right that private schools don't risk offering even modest departures from the "tried and true" academic packages offered by public schools.

However, our school case studies call into question some of the assumptions held by proponents of freer markets in educational services and school choice programs with regard to the perceived advantage of the private sector to organize itself around academic goals and greater client responsiveness.

The public schools in lower-income settings that we visited placed the improvement of their academic record as a top priority. Access to alternative financial resources, the potential to collaborate with social service agencies, a willingness to experiment with alternative novel approaches, and, certainly, increased governmental pressure to demonstrate academic progress have put student learning at the top of the public school agenda. Private schools in socioeconomically disadvantaged areas were more likely to offer educational services structured around a religious mission or the provision of more orderly classrooms to families seeking a safer, more disciplined environment. Private schools appealed to parents less through building reputations for producing high levels of achievement in standard math or language skills and more through their capacity to produce nonachievement educational services, like safety. More importantly, this finding suggests that markets are not sufficient to promote or generate high achievement. For schools to align themselves with producing more learning based predominantly on market forces, parents must demand (and have a clear notion of what constitutes) high academic performance.

Our data also present a contrasting picture to the characterization of the private sector as more responsive and adaptable to consumers. The ability of parents to influence what happens in private schools appears to be greatest at the moment of their initial choice of educational establishment or if they exercise the option to exit to an alternative school. The extent to which their voices can shape school policy while they are active consumers of school services is limited. Private schools, both in higher- and lower-income communities, have proved to be effective in setting up boundaries for parental involvement and decision making. Families often are limited in their ability to modify the package of educational services that private schools provide or the way that it is delivered. In some instances, it could be argued that, in fact, private schools may attempt to hold parents accountable for supporting the school's educational mission, rather than parents holding schools accountable for their children's academic success.

Private schools are constructed around a specific mission or vision that is often not subject to discussion or modification by parents. This is particularly obvious in the case of religious schools, and it makes sense. Catholic schools, for example, were set up not to provide a safer environment than the public schools or to do a better job of teaching reading or arithmetic, but rather to provide Catholic children with a Catholic educational experience in a society dominated by Protestant values and norms (see Bryk, Lee, and Holland, 1993). Yet the explicit spiritual mission of parochial schools is nonetheless at variance with the ambitions and expectations of many parents who send their children to them. This simple truth, however, has sometimes been lost in today's public debates, whether regarding philanthropic plans to fund scholarships for poor non-Catholic children to attend Catholic schools or in legal battles regarding whether tax dollars can properly fund educational vouchers in religious establishments.

Parental voice can take on a very different character in public sector schools. Where parents are highly educated and motivated, they can constitute an effective pressure group that expects to be heard and can insist that schools address their interests and concerns. They can mobilize effectively to command attention and bring about change. As constituents of a public institution, parents have a right to make demands and they are entitled to a response.

In summary, our case studies indicate that privatization and market accountability are not necessarily the solution to improving the public education system. There are two reasons for this. Private schools do not appear to present a more systematic advantage for enhanced effectiveness than public schools. Thus, there is little evidence that increasing the number of private schools will necessarily mean more good models. Private schools in our sample also appeared to have an advantage in the competition for students by offering nonacademic products (religion, safety, or a language immersion program) that differentiate them from their public counterparts. The differentiation of a proeduct mix, however, says little about the delivery of more academic learning. The message that stands out from our research is that poorly run schools can equally use well-run private *and* public schools as reform models.

[4]

THE ORGANIZATION OF SCHOOLING IN PUBLIC AND PRIVATE SCHOOLS

Private sector management is gaining increasing popularity as a proposed remedy for the ailments of the education system. Many education reform advocates have turned their eyes to the private sector in a search for models to emulate to bring about a transformation in failing public schools. Private schools are propounded to be more efficient, less costly, and more productive (in terms of student achievement) than their public counterparts. The engine behind the superiority of private management is ascribed to school choice and a decentralized decision-making style that permits private schools to be more adaptable and attuned to customer needs. Public schools, in turn, are characterized as bogged down in bureaucratic requirements and top-down decision making. Steered by bureaucratic principles, public schools have allegedly grown inflexible, ineffective, and wasteful of resources.

Advocates of privatization and markets in education posit that the failure of public schools stems from lack of competition. The public monopoly in education strangles improvement and originality, applying the same standard approach indistinct of the needs and characteristics of the communities that schools serve. According to Perelman, "the public school is America's collective farm. Innovation and productivity are lacking for largely the same reasons they were scarce in Soviet agriculture: absence of competitive, market forces" (Perelman, 1992, p. 225).

According to educational choice models, the market obliges the private sector to operate in a dynamic environment founded on two key principles: student performance and parent satisfaction. This setting differs vastly from the operational backdrop of government schools, in which politics and bureaucratic principles rule supreme. Thus, private schools adopt a distinct organization that distinguishes them from government schools. Private schools are shaped by the rules of the market. Political interests fashion public schools.

From this institutional perspective, public educational practice is under the stronghold of formal regulations and bureaucratic hierarchies to allow for the flexibility and proficiency schools require to thrive and excel. As Chubb and Moe (1990) argue, public schools must contend with a world of rules imposed by local, state, and federal authorities.

Private schools, to the contrary, are ostensibly free to do as they best see fit to design and provide their educational programs. They have a great deal more discretion in terms of shaping their educational offer and its delivery for several reasons. First, they attract a clientele that shares similar interests and aspirations; hence they are less mired in conflict and negotiation. Second, private schools are not bogged down by public bureaucracies. Third, markets steer the private sector to seek out innovation, implement best practice models, attract high-quality staff, and adopt research-based curricula and instructional methods (Lips, 2000).

If in fact private and public schooling were closely aligned along these variables, the differences between these sectors would be easily detected. We would find private schools organized around market-driven demands. On the other hand, public schools would be shaped by bureaucratic forces. Specifically, public schools would be expected to show little specialization and great homogeneity across environments. Public employee protections and unionizations would foster laxity in teacher standards and performance, while management practices would be clearly bounded by bureaucratic regulations. Public schools ought to be bogged down by centrally driven requirements, such as curricular mandates, lesson plan registers, teacher evaluation procedures, and the like, that bind the work of educators and ultimately constrict their capacity to adapt school norms and direct classroom activities to the particular needs of their student population. Conversely, private schools would be free of such exigencies and would enjoy greater discretion to assess and determine what kind of school organization and classroom behavior best suit the pupils that they serve. There should be evidence of a greater variety of teaching approaches, curricula, instructional methods, and education philosophies among private establishments. Management practices in the private sector should also reflect a lean apparatus motivated by high standards and adaptability. Staff performance would be measured in relation to clear guidelines and linked to rewards and punishments.

Our case studies, however, portray another picture altogether. In terms of their organization, the public and private schools visited were remarkably similar. In the absence of clear religious imagery, an unknowing visitor would have found it hard to guess the nature of any given school's funding on the basis of classroom-related activities. The first section of this chapter explores the conditions of teaching in schools with regard to selection, professional development, evaluation, and dismissal. The second section describes the character of the academic program in public and private schools, with particular reference to academic flexibility and innovation, curricular programs, pedagogical philosophy, and classroom management practices. The final section posits that the public–private dichotomy is not an instructive theory for understanding how schools organize themselves to deliver schooling services. Public and private schools can be equally subject to bureaucratic rules and regulations. More importantly, academic innovation, curricular flexibility, and exemplary instances of teaching and learning practices span the public and private sectors alike.

THE CONDITIONS OF TEACHING

The conditions of teaching in private schools are often described as freer from constraints, but under close observation both environments are organized around fairly uniform structural and normative criteria, such as subjects, class periods, classroom rules, and so on. Children may be sitting in groups around a table or frontally behind individual desks, but the technology of teaching and learning is much alike in the public and private domains. All educators face equally the pressures from standardized tests and struggle with striking a balance in the amount of class time dedicated to readying students for these exams and embracing broader academic goals. And educators must equally abide by public regulations concerning health, safety, and civil rights. Yet most teachers in public and private schools are also able to exercise a significant degree of autonomy and discretion behind the closed door of their classrooms.

There seems to be a widely held belief that one of the most important differences between public and private schools is the laxity of teacher standards stimulated by public employee protections and unionization. This important distinction ought to trigger visible variations in teacher recruitment and retention, hiring standards, performance evaluation, and dismissals. Our observations, however, suggest otherwise.

TEACHER RECRUITMENT AND RETENTION

There is no apparent distinction in the ability of public and private schools to attract suitable candidates for their teacher cadre. Some teachers argue that they seek out schools where students come from fairly advantageous backgrounds, while others emphasize their desire to work in underprivileged communities. For some teachers, a commitment to their school's particular pedagogical approach or spiritual philosophy is an important determinant of their place of work. A common response among teachers for their choice of workplace is often related to their finding a tight-knit, congenial, professional environment. This sense of collegiality may be nourished by a wide variety of factors. In many schools, the principal plays a key role in fostering reflection, professional exchanges, and personal interaction. In others, schools are purposefully organized to operate largely as a community center where teaching staff work together with other professionals as a team to look after children's socioemotional needs in addition to traditional academic goals. In some other schools, espousing a specific pedagogical approach or academic objective often acts as a rallying principle to bring staff together under a common vision. In all these instances, collegiality has a significant impact on the professional performance of teachers and principals. Much of their devotion and commitment to their students has its footing on the strength and encouragement of a professional peer support network.

These attributes are found in and span across both the public and private sectors. Overall, it could be said that in terms of the likelihood to recruit teachers there is no apparent advantage in either sphere. Both sectors enjoy similar benefits and face similar constraints in their ability to offer sufficiently attractive conditions to their teaching staff.

With regard to teacher selection and retention, a severe teacher shortage has greatly affected the ability of public and private educational establishments to recruit qualified instructors. This constraint was perhaps most clearly felt in lower-income schools where the conditions of teaching and learning present significant challenges. Principals assumed that the most academically skilled teachers would not be available to them in all probability. This was especially noted in private schools (both secular and religious), where salary scales were generally lower compared to those at public schools and teacher selection could seldom be based primarily on an assessment of teaching skill or curricular approach.

St. Felipe's is a kindergarten through eighth-grade Catholic school operated by Dominican sisters. The principal has directed the school for ten years. She herself attended the school as a child, graduating from eighth grade in 1961. St. Felipe's is located in a primarily African-American suburb. Student enrollment is about 70 percent black and 30 percent Hispanic, practically evenly split between Catholic and non-Catholic children. In addition to regular classes, the school operates a morning care program for children whose parents work, beginning at 6 A.M. (and serving breakfast), as well as an afterschool program until 6 P.M. Parked on the parish grounds is a portable classroom used by a federally subsidized Title I teacher for additional tutoring of eligible children who are having reading difficulties. (Federal regulations require that the space used for Title I programming to be physically separate from the regular school space in a religious school.)

About half of the teaching faculty at St. Felipe's is new each year. The vice-principal attributes this fact primarily to low salaries and the difficulties of teaching unusually difficult children. This year, the third-, fifth-, sixth-, and seventh-grade teachers are new, and the second- and fourth-grade teachers are in their second year. This substantial turnover makes the operation of St. Felipe's very difficult. Because there are always so many inexperienced teachers on staff, a great deal of the time and energy of the principal and the experienced teachers are expended in training new teachers in the basics of maintaining discipline and order in a difficult environment, leaving little time or energy for making improvements in the academic program. The vice-principal herself is leaving at the end of this year to work in a public school because she feels that she can no longer work at the low salary scale for teachers provided at St. Felipe's.

At Knuckleborough, a for-profit school serving lower middle- and middle-income students, the original proprietor had an explicit policy of keeping salaries low and class sizes small. The owner believed that he could offset the teacher quality loss from low salaries, first, by investing heavily in professional development for teachers and, second, by benefiting from the enthusiasm that young new teachers would bring to the job. This enthusiasm, he reasoned, would offset teachers' lack of skill and experience. The present proprietor has maintained low salaries, but she drastically reduced the investment in professional development. The result is a 40 percent annual turnover rate in the teaching faculty, across the school's eighteen full-time classroom teachers and six area specialists. When we asked parents, teachers, and administrators what accounted for this phenomenon, they included such things as low pay, lack of professional growth, depressing facilities, and noise level as contributing factors. The school librarian, one of the more veteran of staff members, went as far as to list low salaries as the single most important factor contributing to the high teacher turnover at Knuckleborough. Teachers usually find placement within the local school district after 1 or 2 years of service.

The frequent pattern across these schools is one in which young teachers gain their initial work experience teaching in the private sector and later apply for positions at public schools because of the pay differentials. A migration from private to public establishments was not uncommon in the schools observed.

On the other hand, many teachers express being attracted to schools for nonmonetary reasons. For instance, teachers at St. Milton's and St. Donat's highlight that they have opted to teach in an inner-city Catholic school rather than migrate to a better-paying post at a public school because of a more attractive working environment than that offered in government schools. At St. Barbara's, a teacher in a neighboring public school was recruited when the principal became impressed with the preparation of first graders who transferred to St. Barbara's. As a result, she aggressively pursued the public school's kindergarten instructor, who accepted a position at

St. Barbara's despite a cut in pay because she liked the communal "family" atmosphere she found at this Catholic school.

The private sector schools hold an advantage with regard to their public counterparts in their flexibility to hire potential candidates. Government schools must abide by specific criteria and prerequisites established by school districts and their union contracts. The example of Adams Charter Middle School is illustrative of this situation. Adams Charter was started in 1994 by a group of parents who sought to implement an integrated arts curriculum. In its first year, the school was affiliated with the local County Office of Education. Officially, it operated as a collective of students in a home-schooling program. Unhappy about the traditional middle schools in the area, these parents convinced other parents through meetings and fliers to join them. Adams School became a charter the following year, sponsored by the County Unified School District. The school started with forty-eight students from sixth to eighth grade. One of the founders credits their success to an abiding interest in the town for creating an alternative to the existing large public middle schools, each with 1,200 students. But the school district was initially resistant to the idea of having a small alternative school among the two large middle schools already established in the area; hence, when the school board approved the charter, it did so only under the condition that the school would fall under the California Educational Code. In California, local school districts must approve and sponsor a charter. Adams Charter, consequently, has less autonomy from the district than parents would like. Because it is obliged to answer to the mandates of the local district, Adams Charter is considered to have a weak charter.

Charter schools usually enjoy great latitude in selecting their staff but, since Adams Charter is obliged to follow the California Educational Code, the school can only hire credentialed teachers registered at the district applicants' pool. During its first year of operation, the principal, not knowing that she could not conduct an independent search, put an ad in a major national newspaper. One of the teachers explains what ensued: "We got applicants from everywhere. It was amazing. People were coming from everywhere because they were interested in the small size [of the school]. . . . The district was furious. . . . What happened is we ended up bringing a lot of people into the school district. Those people that came to apply for the job had to actually register [with the district]."

For the following few years, the district sought to exercise its right to assign teachers directly. School administrators were invited to participate in the interview process, but they had limited decision-making faculties. This was cause for a lot of dissatisfaction. According to parents, the district appointed teachers to Adams Charter who were left over from all the other public schools in the area. One of the school founders expressed the hardships that they experienced in the early years of the school and her disapprobation of the school staff in this manner:

> We couldn't have the teachers that we really wanted to have. We got competent teachers but they really weren't aligned with the vision of the school and they weren't necessarily the most creative thinkers. We were looking for people who really thought outside the box, who were not logged into the system, who were willing to take some risks in dealing with the curriculum. I find the more you look the more you have to go outside the system to really locate these people.

Over the years, the district has relaxed its stance and Adams Charter has regained greater control over the teacher hiring process. District control, however, still extends to the teacher evaluation process. Due to the fact that the principal is not a certified administrator, she cannot formally appraise teachers. Hence, another principal appointed by the school district must come periodically to the school to assess teacher performance. Not surprisingly, the evaluation of teachers by an authority figure from without the school community is a source of tension, particularly in light of the fact that district and school goals and expectations differ.

HIRING STANDARDS AND TEACHER QUALITY

As the case of Adams Charter illustrates, schools strive to hire candidates that subscribe to their philosophy or vision. When asked what they sought in teacher candidates, charter school principals emphasized qualities related to the school's overarching educational approach. Olympic Charter, for instance, looks for teacher candidates who believe in focused individualized instruction for each child, allowing children to develop and learn at their own pace. A developed understanding of constructivism is not required, as indoctrination in these methods intensifies once a teacher joins the staff.

A committee of teachers, parents, and the principal conducts the teacher screening process at Olympic. Candidates are recruited through advertisements as well as by word-of-mouth referrals from existing teachers. In several instances, recent graduates who had student-taught at Olympic were hired for vacancies. The selection committee then interviews the candidates for the position, reviews résumés, and checks references. Although the selection committee is formally responsible for teacher hiring, all teachers and parents may participate in the initial interviews. In one case, a teacher reported being confronted with a panel of thirty-five teachers and parents, all of whom, as she recalls, posed sophisticated questions. Because each teacher "team-teaches" with a partner in a double-class cluster, Olympic has a policy that the ultimate decision about teacher selection lies with the partner teacher in whose classroom the vacancy occurs. Virtually every young teacher we interviewed reported that she is now a better teacher because she has grown professionally from the peer collaboration around which Olympic is organized.

In the case of public schools, principals were more likely to emphasize pedagogical skill and academic qualifications in their teacher selection procedures. The school head at Mashita, for example, noted that candidates are evaluated on how they respond to questions about classroom technique or pedagogical philosophy. At Renaissance, a school reconstituted because of its poor track record in student achievement measures, the principal was brought in with a mandate to turn around a failing school. He was given the opportunity to hire an entire staff and to recruit from outside the district and the state. In recruiting teachers, the principal set specific expectations for candidates. In a letter to all applicants, he described the qualities of a good candidate, including "a commitment to developing student self-esteem through successful experiences and positive relationships." Similarly, at United, another elementary school serving primarily lower income children, the principal sought to attract teachers able to educate "the whole child" and demonstrate an understanding of the connection between academic success and other social aspects of students' lives.

Private school principals also strive to strike a balance between teaching skill and affective–personal characteristics in teacher applicants. In low-income religious schools, a strong spiritual belief system is often deemed an important prerequisite for employment. For example, St. Jeremy's Lutheran School recruits teachers almost exclusively from the synod's teacher colleges. Graduates from these training institutions usually have studied an academic major and a religion minor. In the few cases when a teacher was recruited from elsewhere, St. Jeremy's expected the teacher to take religion in-service courses. According to St. Jeremy's principal, prospective teachers are evaluated on "their allegiance to the faith, their doctrinal understanding." Inquiries into candidates' pedagogical philosophy are secondary, as the principal stated, because the school had adopted an explicit curriculum guide and teachers needed only to follow it.

Like her counterpart at St. Jeremy's, the principal at St. Felipe's remarked that she is primarily interested in a prospective teacher's family background and religious orientation: "I'm not saying that they have to be Catholic, but I think it's important if they are going to teach here, that they . . . really believe in God." Only if this condition is fulfilled does the principal ask the candidate to teach a sample lesson. At St. Barbara's, another Catholic school serving largely a working-class community, the principal argued that the most important component of the teacher interview process was questions about how instructors would handle hypothetical disciplinary problems in the classroom. Next in importance was the teacher's personal religious practice.

In contrast, the school principals of St. Milton's and St. Donat's underscored that a good rapport with children is the most important quality in their hiring decisions. They often examine prospective teachers' academic records to determine whether the candidate has taken courses in child development. At St. Donat's, a religious school serving primarily a Latino community, the Office of Catholic Schools bears the responsibility to prescreen all applicants for teaching jobs in the local archdiocese. Their personnel department checks teacher credentials and qualifications or, if necessary, performs the necessary background security checks. The actual hiring, however, is the responsibility of Sister Meghan, the school principal.

Sister Meghan places great weight on staff selection, and her policies reflect the importance of community spirit and community building at St. Donat's. Candidates are invited to the school for a whole day in order to assess whether they will fit into this tight-knit professional environment. Hiring determinations are usually made jointly by teachers and administrators. As Sister Meghan recounted,

> I think you really have to look to someone who buys into your philosophy. And someone who really cares for children, I mean really cares for children. It's not a job. It has to be a ministry. They have to be dedicated to it. You can pretty well tell that I've been interviewing for twenty-four years. I can tell right away whether this person is "yes" or "no, I know I'm not going to hire this person."
>
> I like to invite them in when I have the opportunity. . . . But I'd like the person to come and spend time in the school, teach, mingle with the staff,

and get input from the staff. "What do you think about [this candidate]? Do you think they'd be a good team member?". . . . And then you get really good feedback from the staff. Sometimes they see things that I don't see, and vice versa. And then [I bring them to] the grade level that they would be working in, I bring those teachers in for part of the interview so that they can explain what they're doing. . . . My first measure is do they really like children? If they don't like children, if they really don't care for children, then I just would not hire them. And you can pick that up. And you see how children act around them, too.

At Shalom Ieladim, a Jewish school in an affluent suburb, teachers are fully responsible for selecting prospective teachers. Pedagogical concerns are in this case a salient selection criterion for prospective teachers. As the principal explained,

I set up a situation in the school where no teacher comes into the school unless all the teachers have seen them teach, have interviewed them, and we agree that this would be an asset to the faculty. So every teacher who comes into this school feels [they] are excellent teachers, as well as I feel that. In fact, what I basically do is I bring maybe three candidates that I think would be excellent for the school. Then we put them through this testing and interview process. So, when I hire a teacher, I feel this is someone who can bring something really good to the school.

The peer selection of staff is also instrumental in creating a tight feeling of community among teachers. An upper-grade teacher reflects that this approach to staff hiring creates a cohesive teacher group "because in the end [the principal] can always say: you chose her. It wasn't me imposing this person upon you. You chose her so let's work with this." Moreover, the current hiring practices impart a sense of security to newcomers. As one newly hired teacher noted, "when the other teachers saw me, they were confident enough in my abilities at that point that I could either learn more or get to a point that I didn't have to feel I had to prove myself."

As the state of California strives to implement its class-size reduction policy in grades K to 3, principals in both the public and private sectors note that teacher shortages have had a serious impact on standards for staff selection. Thus, at Mashita Middle School, while the principal states that she values first and foremost pedagogical philosophy and skill in selecting teachers, she must now select from a pool of uncredentialed teachers who possess insufficient background to answer pedagogical questions. Instead, she evaluates candidates primarily on the basis of interpersonal factors: how well the candidate relates to her or how enthusiastic and self-confident the candidate appears. The principal's view is that teaching requires interpersonal skills, and this may be the best proxy for professional capacity, given the fact that the applicant pool consists almost entirely of candidates without experience. The principal estimates that, at most, she has dismissed about 20 percent of the probationary teachers hired because they were inadequate to the job. In almost all cases, their inadequacy consisted of an inability to maintain control in their classrooms.

The impact of supply-and-demand factors for teachers is perhaps most dramatically illustrated by Liniers French School. Here, for teachers of the French curriculum, the school may receive about one hundred applications from French nationals seeking a teaching experience in the United States. The school sifts through the applications and then interviews the finalists and conducts its selection process in Paris. For American teachers of the English curriculum, however, the Liniers French School faces the same problems as do other private schools in California. Liniers' salaries are considerably less than public school salaries, so the statewide teacher shortage causes the school to have great difficulty attracting highly qualified applicants.

STAFF PERFORMANCE EVALUATION

Despite the importance ascribed to continuous teacher performance monitoring as a means for professional development and quality control by principals and educators alike, it seldom took place in practice in the schools we observed. This is true for schools in both the public and private sectors. A common explanation as to why teacher evaluations received such little attention was that principals had too many other responsibilities to devote significant time to this critical aspect of instructional supervision. The tasks that consumed much of the principals' time were quite diverse. In the larger public schools, administrative tasks and disciplinary concerns took most of the principal's time. In smaller private schools, especially those in low-income communities, fund-raising and tuition negotiations with families experiencing financial difficulties were frequently cited. The principal at United summarized her experience with the following words:

> I feel I'm supposed to be the instructional leader, which I try to be, but there's little time for that to be real honest with you. Most of the time I'm also responsible for the building, for the personnel, for the budget, for everything. I mean, the parents, any problems that happen here. Funding, I have to look for funding, and the district paperwork. I don't have an assistant and we have over 700 kids.

At public schools, state law requires that probationary teachers receive a formal evaluation each year and that tenured teachers be appraised every 2 years. Some teachers, however, reported that formal evaluations took place as rarely as once every 3 years. When evaluations did take place, they were conducted in a rather "mechanistic" fashion, as a fulfillment of an established obligation, rather than as a reflective exercise in its own right.

Evaluations usually begin with a notification to the teacher that the principal plans to observe a classroom lesson. Teacher performance is appraised against a standardized form in which a range of teacher and classroom characteristics is listed. Following the observation, the teacher discusses the outcomes of the appraisal with the principal and then signs the evaluation in agreement. This was the case for a working-class public school like Mashita, the reconstituted Renaissance Middle School, or the resource-wealthy Tatuna

Point, and in low-income Catholic schools like St. Felipe's and St. Milton's, at the for-profit Knuckleborough, or at Liniers French School.

At Ayacucho, teachers are supposed to be formally evaluated once a year by the principal. While every educator seemed aware of the evaluation process, only the newer teachers reported being evaluated on a regular basis. One teacher recalled having been evaluated only twice in 5 years. The main function of these evaluations is allegedly to help new teachers to improve their teaching skills, but the intended effect is not always achieved through this means. As a fourth-grade teacher explained,

> We use [standardized evaluation] packets, which have categories like "teacher as planner," "teacher as decision-maker," and so on. We are supposed to sit down with the principal and go over these packets. But it doesn't really happen. The principal is supposed to go over these packets. I've had only one formal evaluation in over 2 years of teaching here. I don't know if I even have a written assessment.

In the case of St. Felipe's, a representative of the Dominican sisters visits the school periodically to make an evaluation. This is not an annual occurrence, but rather it takes place every 2 years or so. In addition, archdiocesan policy requires the principal to conduct a formal evaluation of teachers twice a year, once in the fall semester and once in the spring. Following the second observation, a meeting is arranged to discuss teacher performance. Sister Deborah, the principal, confessed that she is usually unable to complete these evaluations. There are inevitably scheduling problems or other responsibilities take precedence. This year, for example, she was able to conduct a formal observation in only six of the school's nine classrooms during the fall semester. As one experienced teacher described this evaluation process, "other things tend to get in the way and [the evaluation] is more like something Sister has to do rather than something she's excited about doing."

Yet it would be inaccurate to characterize principals as disengaged from what occurs in the classroom. Teachers are usually appraised and receive feedback on their performance in an informal manner. At Knuckleborough, according to the faculty handbook, the director has the responsibility to conduct an annual "formal" evaluation. As a lower-grade teacher admitted, this formal evaluation was not considered to be very effective. "I don't know how much you can learn from a 10-minute observation. I think you really need to be there a long time." Instead, it is the director's casual observations and informal dialogue that are deemed more informative. An upper-grade teacher made the following remarks:

> [The director] always knows what's going on with what you're teaching. She'll make a lot of questions about what's going on, all in a pretty informal way. "You're teaching this book, have you thought about doing this or that?" That's always been pretty helpful. I asked her if she would come team-teach a short-story creative writing lesson because I wanted to watch her teach and also have her watch me do some stuff. That was actually pretty successful and enjoyable. But, again, these kinds of things, you know, it's informal and just done on a casual basis.

At United Primary School, the district-mandated teacher evaluation procedure consists of a scheduled principal observation of a 40-minute lesson. In the case of new teachers, evaluations are expected to take place three to four times a year, with a meeting between the principal and the teacher before and after the observation. In the premeeting, the teacher reviews the goals of the lesson, and in the postmeeting the two discuss how the lesson went and any improvements that the teacher might be able to make. Every teacher interviewed, however, commented on the principal's daily presence in the classrooms as a more effective feedback mechanism than the formal evaluation procedure. These continuous observations and discussions allow for more formative and thoughtful evaluations of the United teaching staff. Teachers reckoned that their classroom doors are always open and, since the principal comes through them regularly, they can obtain ongoing feedback year round. The district procedure has become largely a formality.

At St. Barbara's, the principal sought to turn the ritualized evaluation protocol common to the archdiocese and public school districts into a more useful exercise. Several years ago, she videotaped each teacher as part of the annual evaluation. The videotape was then used as an instrument so that teacher and principal could jointly explore strengths and weaknesses. This procedure, though, was not well received. Teachers objected to being videotaped; hence, the principal ceased this practice for the moment. She hopes to resume this type of evaluation some time in the future.

But a heavy administrative burden, whether to fulfill district obligations in public schools, to respond to parental demands in high-income establishments, or to attend to fund-raising needs in inner-city Catholic schools, usually prevents principals from having sufficient time to devote to the formative evaluation of the teacher cadre. Sister Deborah, the principal of St. Milton's, for instance, is constantly in and out of classrooms. But her energies are frequently directed to resolving fights between children, helping to settle down unruly students, or counseling a child with emotional difficulties. Sister Deborah is intimately aware of her students' emotional development and disciplinary problems, and she has a clear sense of her teachers' strengths and weaknesses with regard to classroom management as well. But she lacked the time (and perhaps even the inclination) to address pedagogical or curricular issues with her staff.

In the schools we observed, occasions for this sort of advice, although highly valued, were ultimately infrequent. Schools such as Olympic Charter, a public elementary school serving 385 children, appear to be more the exception than the rule. The principal visits each of the school's six classrooms two to three times every day and proposes pedagogical suggestions frequently. Olympic's small size seems to be an important explanatory variable for such close interaction. Teachers found the principal's suggestions very helpful, especially because many of them were experimenting with student-centered approaches unfamiliar to them.

Peer mentoring programs, when properly implemented, acted as an important support network and played a significant role in furthering teacher professional development. Their ability to inspire pedagogical reflection and their effectiveness as a quality control mechanism were judged superior to the formal evaluation system.

A dramatic influx of new staff persuaded the principal of United to develop a mentor teacher program. Each new teacher was assigned to a veteran teacher to ease the transition and share strategies and resources. From their first day in the school, new teachers were matched to a particular individual with whom they could reflect on pedagogical practices and from whom they could learn about overall school procedures. Teachers also met regularly by grade level to discuss teaching strategies and lesson plans. A veteran kindergarten teacher explained how they worked together to assist new staff:

> The kindergarten teachers meet on a weekly basis to share materials, ideas. We meet to develop our thematic teaching units. We especially meet that frequently because we have three new teachers [at] our grade level and it's really hard being brand new and not knowing all the curriculum and all the materials available. . . . We're all kind of mentors for them and help them.

Overall, new teachers appreciated how much they could learn from veteran teachers and acknowledged that being in a mutually supportive environment made all the difference.

St. Jeremy's followed the recommendation of the Lutheran synod to develop a similar peer mentoring scheme. Teachers with no prior experience were matched to teachers with the greatest length of service to serve as mentors. The synod convened workshops for new teachers and then for the mentors, and then both groups were brought together in a third workshop to coordinate this program.

The first-grade teacher was assigned to mentor the newly hired seventh-grade teacher. They describe the mentor's role as primarily being one of providing support. Ms. Calin's class, the veteran teacher, was normally dismissed earlier than the seventh grade; hence, Ms. Calin occasionally looked into the seventh-grade classroom at the end of the day to make sure that everything was going smoothly and to offer help. Similarly, the new fourth-grade teacher was matched to another veteran teacher. She would often receive notes of encouragement and offers to help from her mentor. But, in spite of its good intentions, this program did little to foster a dialogue on pedagogical or curricular matters. The new teachers rarely asked for assistance, and the veteran educators were advised by the synod only to intervene upon solicitation. Their role ought not to be an administrative one. "Unless [teachers] ask for your help, there's really nothing you can do." Later in the year, the synod convened a meeting of mentors and mentees to discuss how the program had functioned. It was agreed that one weakness of the program was that it depended too much on new teachers asking their mentors for help, when it was sometimes the case that new teachers needed help without being aware of the need or that they were simply afraid to come forward and ask for assistance, even of their designated mentor.

Several other schools had implemented to larger or lesser degrees teacher mentoring programs. At Shalom Ieladim, teachers were paired into a combined classroom. This created a structure in which every teacher, new or old, could be complemented by another who might have different strengths and weaknesses. In other schools, such as St. Milton's, teachers acknowledged receiving little assistance from their mentor, but were nonetheless grateful for the fact that the mentor was available if needed. How well a mentor system works often depends on the personalities and inclinations of the teachers involved. A feeling of isolation is not uncommon among teaching staff. A teacher who had decided to leave Knuckleborough and had been interviewing with private and public schools in the area summarized his experience in one succinct critical comment: "I'm finding out maybe that [the lack of professional training and support] is kind of more typical than I thought. I thought it was really, you know, just Knuckleborough that didn't have the formal structure. But, I'm looking at other places—public and private—seeing that no one's really got that structure. I have to get my expectations in order."

DISMISSAL POLICIES

The voluntary departure and dismissal of school staff is an indication of the caliber of a school's instructional cadre and the standards used to monitor teacher performance. An obvious distinction between public and private institutions lies in the power of private schools to fire teachers. The tenure system in public education makes the removal of a classroom instructor an arduous procedure, even for charter schools. Union contracts are deemed to burden public schools with poor-performing educators. The private sector, instead, is allegedly free to abide by clear performance standards and purge those teachers who are not performing adequately or who do not fit in with the school's culture.

Indeed, dismissals in the public sector are more the exception than the rule. Yet most schools emphasize that this is not a reflection of a laxity of standards in the public sector. At United, the formal district evaluation procedure is often described as a formality. However, when teachers do not perform up to the school's expectations, there are real and obvious consequences. "I really do not want to keep teachers on staff who I feel are not good for the kids," underscored the principal. Last year one teacher was asked to leave because the principal considered that she was not doing an adequate job.

In her brief tenure at Olympic Charter School, the principal stated that she has never felt it to be necessary to fire a teacher as a result of an unsatisfactory evaluation. In fact, she was enthusiastic, without exception, about her entire staff. But prior to her arrival, Olympic faced a problem with unsatisfactory teachers. Strong due-process protections in the school district made it difficult to fire them. In one case, an instructor was generally known not to be working hard in the classroom and frequently leaving school early. Little could be done about this until the teacher was caught giving answers to students during a district-wide standardized test. At this point, the teacher was forced to leave. In another case, a teacher had an open affair with the husband of a teacher's aide at the school. The teacher's transfer to another school was arranged. This is a common approach espoused in cases when gross incompetence or immoral conduct is not involved. The principal had to devise ways of pressuring the teacher into transferring out to a different school without penalty.

Parental pressures can play a significant role in terminating the professional relationship of a staff member with a school. This is most obvious in higher-income communities, where parents feel more at ease making their views known to school or district leaders. In Adams Charter, like other charter schools, the charter council does not formally oversee school staff. The principal and teachers are officially supervised by the school district. The nature of permanent and close parental participation in all aspects of school life, however, does foster a strong accountability system that may circumvent traditional limitations in the enforcement of state regulations and standard district accountability. This informal accountability system can carry great weight. In recent years, an upper-grade teacher was asked to leave the school. The decision did not originate from the district that formally supervised her work, but rather from continuous parental pressure to have her dismissed.

Teacher contracts can be terminated more easily at a private school. Yet teacher dismissals were also a largely extraordinary event in the schools we visited. There was no indication that private schools applied a different or more rigorous set of standards than did their public counterparts. The principal at St. Donat's explained why she "never had to fire a teacher" in the following terms. Formal evaluations are not really the conduit to weed out poor educators. The pay is low, the hours are long, and the teaching conditions are far from optimal. Teachers who are not truly committed to teaching most often leave on their own accord after 1 or 2 years of service.

As in the public school sector, some evidence suggests that bureaucratic regulations and fear of judicial action might encourage a reluctance to dismiss unsatisfactory teachers in the Catholic school system. Catholic elementary schools are not formally accountable to the archdiocesan school department. In principle, each parish is independent in its control over parish schools. Yet the archdiocese in practice exercises strong control over parish elementary schools, coordinating curriculum, testing, budgeting, and, most dramatically, personnel policies. In cases where low-income schools receive an archdiocesan subsidy, the control is more formalized. The principal at St. Barbara's, for instance, remarked that the archdiocese had vast influence in their decision making. "They monitor and they outline every move we make. We are always accountable to them."

Bureaucratic control of local Catholic elementary schools is clearest with regard to personnel determinations. Archdiocesan policy is that its lawyers will represent any parish school whose administrators abide by archdiocesan legal advice. Schools habitually would not consider functioning without this safety net. Thus, the Catholic school principals we interviewed underscored that they would not take significant personnel actions without consulting first with their archdiocesan elementary school supervisor.

In general, archdiocesan supervisors were conservative in their advice. Although there is no tenure system in Catholic schools, fear of lawsuits from discharged teachers is an ever-present motif guiding policy. Archdiocesan personnel handbooks set forth rules of progressive and consistent disciplinary measures for teachers, nearly as restricting as the policies of unionized public school districts. Potential discharge cases are seldom approved by the archdiocese, because they rarely meet the standards of due process required by archdiocesan policies. In practice, Catholic school principals approach unsatisfactory teachers in much the same way that public school principals do: admit complacency or engage in a policy of subtle harassment in hope that the unsatisfactory teacher will resign.

St. Felipe offers an interesting example. A teacher was taunted by some high school students as she drove home. The teacher allegedly got out of her car and struck one with the heel of her shoe, causing injury. The teacher was arrested, but the archdiocese advised the principal that she could take no action unless there was a conviction. Even though teachers at St. Felipe's are hired on annual contracts, the school did not believe that it could risk dismissing this educator while the criminal case was pending for fear of a lawsuit.

In another instance, after investigating several parent complaints, the principal became dissatisfied with the instructional competence of a teacher. The principal, however, had not documented the warnings and observations necessary to meet the due process requirements outlined in the personnel handbook. The strategy employed by the principal was to relieve the teacher of her responsibilities for managing the student snack shop, a duty the principal knew that the teacher enjoyed. The teacher became angered and told the principal she was quitting. The principal accepted the resignation on the spot. Later, when the teacher calmed down and reconsidered, the principal got support from the archdiocese for refusing to permit the teacher to rescind her resignation.

In two different Catholic schools we observed, unmarried teachers became pregnant. In each case, the principal and pastor thought that the teacher should be fired because teachers' contract included a stipulation that they lead a "moral life." In neither case did the schools obtain archdiocesan approval to act on this wish. The teachers remained full-time employees at these schools.

Teacher dismissals seemed more likely to take place when teachers were still within their probationary period. In twelve years, Sister Sue, the principal at St. Milton's, terminated one teacher only. The educator in question was warm and caring toward the children but, despite having her teaching credential, could not organize a lesson. The children began to become disengaged when bombarded by this disorganized curricular input. Other teachers at St. Milton's had reported to the principal that the new teacher was not effective, that her classroom was unruly, and that the curriculum did not seem to be followed. Parents complained as well, both personally and by sending letters to the school. In addition, the new teacher seemed to have a series of health problems that interfered with her ability to focus and organize her teaching. Sister Sue sponsored the teacher to attend several archdiocesan workshops on the math curriculum and a master teacher worked with her daily. When the master teacher did not seem to be effective in helping the new teacher to improve, Sister Sue asked another experienced teacher to take over the mentoring role. Sister Sue herself worked with the teacher in the classroom, but improvement did not seem to be forthcoming. Twelve weeks into the teacher's first semester, Sister Sue asked for the teacher's resignation.

This discretionary power to terminate a contract during a teacher's probationary period also exists in public schools. All new teachers are effectively on probation for 3 years before being considered for tenure. It is formally relatively simple not to renew a public school teacher's contract during this period.

Finally, parental pressures appear to play a salient role in staffing decisions in private sector schools, as was the case in their public counterparts. When parents at the Liniers French School complained about the lack of rigor in the English program's first-grade curriculum, the principal did not fire the instructor, but rather reassigned her to a kindergarten opening. At St. Jeremy's Lutheran School, parents complained that an instructor was not teaching any math. The school board launched an investigation. Eventually, the teacher was fired for failing to comply with the school's core religious values and obligations. The teacher had not fulfilled a commitment to attend church services on Sundays. His contract was consequently not renewed under this proviso.

Overall, teacher dismissals were for the most part rare events. Firing a teacher, whether in a public or a private school, is a discretionary power that is exercised warily. An important distinction between these two sectors, however, remains. In public schools, dissatisfied public school teachers can often utilize contractual rights to transfer to another school. Private school teachers do not enjoy this privilege. This lack of options may induce an unsatisfactory teacher to resist, to a greater extent than would be the case in a public school, the pressures to leave.

THE CHARACTER OF THE ACADEMIC PROGRAM

Public and private schools are frequently characterized as possessing different levels of influence over curricular programs and classroom management practices. Public schools must necessarily follow direction from the state department of education, local school boards, and district staff. They are bounded by the rules and regulations that originate at the central office. On the other hand, the private sector is described as enjoying greater autonomy in areas such as determining content and skills to be taught, selection of textbooks and other instructional materials, or implementing alternative teaching techniques. Private schools may change and adapt their style to fit local realities and address the "real" needs of students. Site-based management and local decision making are often advocated as essential ingredients to improving school effectiveness.

Indeed, district and state guidelines play an important role in shaping the academic program of public schools. State competency-based curricular objectives and district subject frameworks matter. They supply a guiding map for teachers to rely on to traverse through the academic year. Mandatory standardized testing also exerts a commanding influence at the classroom level. Such testing sends clear signals of what teachers ought to focus on and the types of skills and understanding that children ought to demonstrate. Together, these central mandates can structure what takes place in the classroom to a significant extent.

Yet this image of a standard program applied indiscriminately across schools, with little regard to the needs of particular children, is misleading. It was not unusual for districts and public schools in our sample to experiment with new approaches. Several schools were engaged in explicit comprehensive attempts to amend their curricular program or had looked into new pedagogical approaches in a search for more effective teaching and learning opportunities for children.

THE PROCESS OF ACADEMIC TRANSFORMATION IN THREE PUBLIC SCHOOLS

It is not surprising that charter schools would enjoy substantial freedom to experiment with alternative educational programs, curricular frameworks, and teaching approaches. Olympic Charter, for instance, distinguishes itself by its constructivist pedagogical philosophy. The school describes itself as a "laboratory school where new ideas are invented, tested and evaluated." As a promotional brochure explains, "The key evidence of the Olympic School's success is visible on a daily basis when one walks through its campus. It is noisy, busy, and unconventional. The students are engaged and highly motivated; the air of discovery, excitement, and learning is unmistakable."

For instance, teachers are encouraged to individualize the curriculum or allow children to work at their own pace.

Likewise, art is the focus of the curriculum at Adams Charter. It is the strongest subject and it serves as a focal point for the academic program schoolwide. As the school plan states, "Adams Charter was founded on a vision: to provide an emotionally and physically safe environment for learning and growing academically, artistically, and personally." The school plan emphasizes two aspects of the curriculum:

1. "A rigorous and challenging curriculum that meets and exceeds the State of California Education Requirements;" and
2. "An integrated, arts-based curriculum that presents information in a connected way so that learning has meaning, cohesion, and depth."

Flexibility in determining school goals and autonomy to shape the academic program are trademarks of the charter school movement. Charter schools were established so as to free schools from the rules and regulations that impede innovation in the public sector. But a similar dynamism and desire for putting into practice educational innovations can also be found in more conventional public schools. The imagery of a public schooled system shackled by bureaucratic norms does not hold true. The following three examples illustrate this point compellingly.

Ayacucho is a Title I elementary school, serving approximately 450 students in grades K to 5. It is located in a low-income Latino community, but administratively is part of a suburban, more affluent school district. Its student population is much more reflective of the neighboring community than of the suburban school district: about half of the school's students is Hispanic, a small percentage is Asian or African American, and the remainder are white. A majority of the students are at-risk. Nearly 80 percent of the students qualify for Title I funds. Ayacucho follows a full-inclusion model whereby special needs students are integrated into regular classrooms.

In the late 1980s, parents staged a "revolt" in order to draw attention to the school's marginality. In response to parental demands, the school principal and, later, the district began to provide Ayacucho with a systematic package of support interventions, including high-quality administration and a well-trained group of teachers—the district pays relatively high salaries—many of who are bilingual. The school currently employs sixteen teachers, as well as a number of special-education and bilingual teacher aides. The school also employs a special projects facilitator to manage its special programs, such as Title I and Title VII, and a community liaison person to develop programs to address the needs of the community.

The school is currently in its fifth and final year of a school-wide restructuring effort. The impetus for the restructuring came from the dissatisfaction of the current principal's predecessor with the low expectations of the district. The former principal explained how the process of change started in the following manner:

> As the principal of the school at the time, I really felt that the expectations of the district were too low. They weren't driving in a direction that I felt they needed to go in order to help the staff to help at-risk kids to be successful. There weren't mechanisms, systems in place to help the school define what it is that they needed to measure. And that's how the restructuring process started. It was by thinking we're here, we know how we are presently measuring it, and it's not showing good results. What are we going to do differently in terms of measurement, instructional strategies, and support systems to make things different?

Approximately 6 years ago, the district appointed a new, dynamic principal at Ayacucho. Until then the district office had been primarily focused on maintaining a smoothly running, financially efficient educational organization. The superintendent at that time had been in place for almost 15 years, and he had made his reputation by keeping the district solvent even as the neighboring district had gone into bankruptcy. School principals were hired for their personnel skills, with little emphasis on educational leadership.

In the face of parental discontent and steering from new leadership, Ayacucho began to transform the educational vision of the school. With the help of the school's leadership team, the principal herself wrote the grant that currently funds the restructuring process. A dramatic transformation ensued that had a tremendous impact on the operations and organization of the school. Traditional teaching methods were replaced in favor of a more child-centered, developmental approach. For reading, phonics-based instruction was replaced with whole-language instruction. In lieu of whole-group instruction and textbooks, teachers turned to cooperative learning and hands-on curriculum. With professional development monies from the restructuring grant, teachers, with the guidance of consultants, began to develop their own thematic curriculum units and to create subject-specific matrices, delineating outcomes that the staff and school administration believed students should reach at each grade level. In keeping with the new developmental philosophy, students were assigned to multiage classrooms, initially with three age groups to a classroom (K–2 and 3–5) and later with two age groups to a classroom (K–1, 2–3, and 4–5). In addition, in an effort to provide students' parents with more information, the school moved from letter-graded to narrative report cards. In the words of one teacher,

> Well, the school has undergone some radical changes over the last 5 years in an attempt to meet the "whole child" and to realize that children learn at different paces, that they use a variety of strategies to learn, that kids have various different strengths. And in doing that they really restructured the environment from being everybody at their desks, using all the old textbooks and only speaking when spoken to, to one with a lot of cooperative grouping, a lot of whole-group things, a lot of hands-on curriculum, a move away from texts, plus the multiage classroom. . . . A lot of energy has been put into developing that approach and making these changes.

In the midst of the school's restructuring process, the district began a transformation of its own. No longer convinced that its schools were doing well, the district embarked on an effort to raise expectations and student achievement in all its schools. A new superintendent with expertise in the area of curriculum and instruction, as well as external pressure from parents and the local business community, caused the district to turn its focus from fiscal and management issues to curriculum and instruction. With support and help from teachers, the district began to develop subject-specific curriculum standards and matrices, which would serve to inform teachers of where their students should be at particular grade levels. It also developed assessments to support the new standards. In addition, the district began providing training and resources to help teachers to use the new system. As one administrator from the district office told us, "If we [the district] are going to have the teachers have hands-on science, we are going to have to build a way for that to happen. We can't just say 'Hey, you're going to do hands-on science.' We provide the training. We provide ways for them to have access to those materials. We provide for people to go by and say 'How are you doing?' "

The teachers at Ayacucho appear to be responding with enthusiasm to the new literacy standards and performance measures supplied by the district. A typical comment was "We are delighted! It's really put that piece into place." Yet, in spite of this dramatic curricular transformation, Ayacucho faces tremendous challenges. To date, the new academic program has had limited impact on enhancing student achievement outcomes. Student test scores continue to be the lowest in the district. In the most recent district language arts assessment, 4 out of 5 first graders, 2 out of 3 second and third graders, and half of fourth graders in the school did not pass. Student learning concerns have gained primacy, yet results have remained elusive.

Renaissance Middle School has also undergone a similar process of profound change with regard to its academic program. During the 1980s, the school district introduced several reform and restructuring strategies in its schools in an effort to provide educational resources and opportunities to traditionally underserved ethnic groups and to raise expectations among educators for children in these groups. This reform package, which was reserved for the lowest-performing schools, combined a number of components into an overall plan for improvement. These included the replacement of existing faculty and staff, selection of a unique instructional focus for each school, high expectations for all students, monitoring student outcomes, extensive professional development, use of technology and flexible class sizes, and parental involvement. This approach to academic transformation was initiated by the school district, but the school and its principal were empowered to design and put into practice their own pathway to promote student academic success.

In a school like Renaissance, which draws on a school population with diverse social needs, getting students to the point where they can focus on learning poses a significant challenge to the staff and leadership of the school. Teachers describe the barriers that students must overcome in their day-to-day lives. Says one, "[I have] learned about the enormous problems these kids come from. Horrific family situations that I've only read about . . . and here it's just a daily thing. And yet these kids can still come to school, semi-function—which is more than I'd be able to do if I came from what they're coming from—laugh, carry on, have goals, have dreams. I think they're amazing!"

The school principal is guided by a model for enhanced learning premised on the fulfillment of basic social and psychological needs. Among these needs, which apply to all endeavors in life, are love and belonging, power, freedom, and fun. Trained in educational psychology, the principal is explicit in his efforts to meet these needs and thus foster learning for all individuals in the school: "The idea is just to embrace all the problems and start dealing with them and eventually the results will be where achievement becomes part of what the kids see as something they need to do. Until they internally feel that way, it's not going to work. I'll have my group of kids that will be successful and then I'll have that big group who won't be successful, unless there's a reason to be successful."

To address the needs of students and to support the individual efforts of teachers, the school has crafted a comprehensive *student care model* designed to monitor students, provide resources and direct interventions in order to address problems in their lives, and institutionalize a culture of caring. The model is best perceived as a layered support network. At the center sits the student, primarily working with classroom teachers. Additional layers focus on solving problems that teachers encounter, helping students to work through issues, and, in some cases, finding alternative settings in which the child can learn. The layers can be accessed as needed and should not be seen as a linear path along which children move as their problems become more serious. Rather, they serve as a series of safety nets to ensure that students do not fall through the cracks.

Classroom teachers provide the primary level of care in the model. Their responsibilities include developing personal relationships with students, tailoring instruction to meet the individual needs of children, recommending additional learning opportunities, maintaining close contact with parents, seeking the advice and support of their colleagues and other professionals in the building, and following through on any plans developed at higher levels of the care system.

But teachers are not alone in their efforts. They receive intensive support from other professionals at the school, including elective teachers (music and physical education), enrichment instructors who provide additional academic training, administrators, security guards, and other support personnel. In addition, by leveraging state and local resources, the school has social workers, a counselor, and a full-time school nurse on staff in the building.

The school is organized into six families, one for each of the three grades (six, seven, and eight), plus special education, bilingual education, and electives. The families are composed of all the teachers in that grade level or subject and are designed to help teachers to collaborate and share information about students. To facilitate this interaction, teachers share students within families. Formally, each family meets at least three times per week to discuss and share information about individual students and to meet with parents. These meetings occur during common planning times and generally last about 1 hour.

Family meetings regularly include other professionals in the school (administrators, social workers, counselors) who can provide insights about students and report on intervention efforts. As a result, there is a diagnostic quality to the meetings, as the group moves from one student to the next, taking input, reviewing progress, exploring alternatives, and reporting on the effectiveness of various strategies.

In their discussions of student needs, teachers and their academic families have significant resources on which to draw. The first floor of the school houses a foundation-funded community center that provides services and activities for students and the Renaissance community at large. Each afternoon, the center runs an afterschool program designed to provide tutoring linked to the school's curriculum, as well as a range of academic and nonacademic activities. In addition, one of the school's social workers has secured state grant money to bolster support for activities related to the physical and emotional well-being of students.

While the student care model is highly developed and includes structured time and support for teachers to address the student issues that arise, the transformation on the curricular program has not yet received the same level of coordination or structural support. The one exception to this general pattern is in the area of mathematics. A basic feature of both the district's curriculum and the school's own approach is teaching students to *understand* mathematics, not just learn the mechanics of it. A teacher explained why she centered her instruction on understanding mathematical concepts in the following terms: "Do you want them to learn how to divide three place numbers into eighteen place numbers, because they're never going to have to do that in their whole lives? Or do you want them to know what division is?"

Despite its extensive freedom to pursue its own academic vision, Renaissance faces an important constraint. It must abide by the district's preoccupation with achievement as measured by standardized test scores (specifically the Comprehensive Test of Basic Skills, or CTBS). A central concern for the district has been the perception that many schools serving African-American and Latino students are plagued by institutionalized racism and low expectations for students. Hence, Renaissance and the other schools in the district are expected to focus its instructional mission on boosting student achievement. "That must be part of our success," said the principal.

The focus on CTBS exerts significant influence on how teachers allocate instructional time. One math teacher dedicates 6 weeks in the spring to CTBS preparation. Another bemoans her inability to get through the district-mandated curriculum, which takes an inquiry approach to mathematics, because of the need to teach arithmetic facts and testing skills. "This district and this school place too much emphasis on CTBS, which is a traditional test. So, after my first year, I really pulled back a lot and said, if they're so concerned, I have to teach traditional math. . . . So, I looked at the curriculum and cut in half what I wanted to do from it to teach arithmetic."

The use of CTBS as a measure of student performance detracts somewhat from that consensus as it blurs signals from the district about how and what teachers should teach. There is some indication that the district is now piloting a new assessment that is more in line with the curriculum.

Changes in student test scores provide some evidence of the transformation that has taken place at Renaissance and a measurable way to monitor progress on the *cognitive* aspects of the school's whole-child approach. Students demonstrated significant gains in reading and mathematics. For the cohort of students that entered sixth grade in the first year after reconstitution, the percentage scoring in the bottom quartile in reading dropped from 44.2 percent to 29.5 percent. In other words, almost 15 percent of these students moved out of the bottom quartile. Similarly, 12.6 percent of this cohort moved out of the bottom quartile in mathematics.

Let's focus now on our third example of innovative practices in public schools. Mashita has 1,700 students in grades 6 to 8. It is part of one of the largest urban school districts in the nation. Its facility is large, including a main building and several portable classrooms perched high on a hill. Between the main building and the other classrooms is a playfield, including a baseball diamond, volleyball nets, and basketball courts drawn onto concrete. Mashita adjoins the campus of the high school that its graduates will attend.

Teachers rely on the state's curriculum framework as their primary guide in designing their academic plans. Textbooks are selected by consensus by the departmental teachers within each grade. They are restricted, however, to books on an approved state list. The state normally pays for all textbooks, and it will not permit state funds to be used for textbooks not on the approved list.

Teachers come together to decide on their textbook choices on the basis of their own appraisals of the quality of the material presented during workshops sponsored by various publishers. In addition, teachers have begun to consider textbook alignment with the standardized assessment instruments adopted by the school district as an important parameter.

Teachers devote considerable effort to developing curriculum materials that will hold children's attention. Field trips and hands-on learning aids have become standard practice across classrooms. Teachers also attend a variety of training workshops to develop their ability to implement such techniques more effectively. Participation in these workshops may be sponsored through federal curriculum reform grants or out of the district's own resources.

Widespread collaboration among teachers on instructional improvement is commonplace. For example, in one case the science, history, and math teachers noticed that the students from a particular English teacher prepared better organized and written reports than students who had had other English teachers. The English teacher in question was then asked to train other teachers, informally, in techniques of teaching writing.

The school has also begun to encourage teachers to work in interdisciplinary teams called pods. This entails scheduling students so that a group of 150 or so share common classes in core subjects. Thus, teachers at a given grade level are organized into pods where history, English, math, and science teachers can meet together to coordinate lesson plans, integrate the curricular programs of the various disciplines, track student progress, and have joint conferences with parents when possible.

Some groups of teachers have been more receptive to this collaborative approach than others; hence, there is wide disparity in the development of pods throughout the school. The mechanics for the implementation of this system are still in a development phase. At the moment of our observations, it had not been possible to schedule all students in a common group. Nor had it been possible to schedule students who share core teachers into common homerooms. Consequently, the goal of "schools within a school," frequently mentioned in middle school reform literature, is still somewhat distant.

The team approach to middle school learning is supported by the school district with training programs for teachers and resource centers equipped with relevant literature and materials. Teams meet every week on a day when the regular school schedule is shortened to allow for such planning. This year, for example, one team planned a schoolwide Civil War pageant in which there was a role for each of the academic disciplines.

In addition, the school administration has sought to emphasize more teacher participation in decision making. The faculty is organized around a number of focus groups that strive to address a variety of problems and projects: parental involvement, improving attendance, reading and literacy, behavior and discipline policies, or sports and the arts program. Teachers agree that these focus groups have made a positive contribution to advancing the school's academic goals and objectives.

In summary, Ayacucho, Renaissance, and Mashita have enjoyed significant leeway to implement their own vision of effective teaching and learning practices. They had significant discretion in putting into place an academic program that responded largely to a school-born programmatic strategy. Districts, for the most part, acted in a largely supportive manner during this change process, either by mobilizing additional resources, providing training opportunities, or supplying technical assistance. But districts also conveyed their academic priorities clearly and laid out specific parameters of what schooling is expected to attain through curricular guidelines and standardized tests. These expectations largely demarcate the boundaries within which public schools operate and conduct their business.

THE QUESTION OF ACADEMIC DIVERSITY AND INNOVATION IN PRIVATE SCHOOLS

Whereas proponents of markets in education hold that public schools function like "antiquated" factories from the "horse-and-buggy" era, private schools are portrayed to be free from the burden of bureaucratic rules and regulations, transforming them into dynamic and innovative environments (Finn, Manno, and Vanourek, 1999). Our case studies, in turn, suggest that the organizational behavior of private schools does not veer significantly from that of their public school counterparts. To a significant extent, private schools operate and are constrained by the very same forces that shape educational academic practices in the public sector: state curricular frameworks and standardized tests.

Every Catholic school in our sample followed a curriculum guide published by the local archdiocese. This guide is published as a scope and sequence manual that specifies both the contents and the number of minutes to be devoted to each academic subject per day. In developing their curricula, the archdioceses relied heavily on the state curriculum frameworks published by the California State Department of Education. As these frameworks also guide the curricula of most public schools, in this respect the guiding principles underlying school curricula were largely comparable. Similarity in curricular contents was reinforced by a similarity in the assessment system espoused in public and private schools. A great number of Catholic schools administered the Stanford Achievement Test to students to monitor student academic progress. This test also receives wide dissemination among public establishments.

At St. Felipe's, the basic curriculum for each grade is set forth in the archdiocesan curriculum manual, which each new teacher receives upon being hired. The manual specifies the contents to be covered in religion, reading, math, and other academic subjects and the number of minutes of instructional time to be devoted to each. Teachers base their weekly lesson plans on this manual and submit these plans to the principal for review.

To promote better intergrade articulation of the curriculum and teaching strategies across grade levels, upper-, mid-, and lower-grade teachers are organized in clusters. This coordinating arrangement does not always operate formally, but the school is small enough that teachers can nonetheless meet informally frequently to discuss students' academic problems or share specific advice on teaching and learning issues.

In the lower grades, St. Felipe's has adopted a computer-based reading support program. This program is managed through the archdiocese. It is mandated as a condition for receipt of a donated computer lab where the program is implemented. The computer lab instructor works under the supervision of the regular lower-grade teachers to assess student progress in reading skills and intensify remedial activity when it is deemed necessary. Classroom teachers confer with the computer lab instructor to determine at what pace each child should be expected to advance and in which programmed instructional package each child should be working. In addition, program consistency is maintained across the archdiocesan low-income schools where the program and computers have been donated. In addition, this program includes a system of "buddy" schools through which the computer teacher and lower-grade teachers meet regularly with their counterparts in another partner school.

In recent months, the archdiocese launched an additional regional activity: a staff development program in mathematics in order to align the curriculum with state standards. According to the principal, however, the program "bombed" because it was based on a cascade model, depending on training lead teachers to instruct other teachers in the new math curriculum. The lead teachers, however, were inadequately prepared for the task. As a result, there was tremendous resistance from the teachers to implement the new mathematics standards. For instance, in the month prior to our school observations, the principal had a faculty meeting in which she attempted to defend the use of calculators in teaching math. The teachers, on the whole, resisted this, believing that until children knew the basics they could never progress further. The principal argued to little avail:

[Students] need to know how to do the function. But when you have a child with a divisor of three digits into a dividend of five—they may never get it. If they have the concept, that's fine. The computation they may never get. That's why they need to learn how to use a calculator. Some children can never get the math computation right away. Maybe high school, maybe, you know, later on. But we need to teach them how to do it. But if they can't do it, we need to say, "Okay, there's the calculator. . . ." Look at yourselves when you balance your checkbook. Are you going to just do it by hand, or are you going to get your little calculator out? So we need to show our children the tools.

As an alternative to this ineffective staff development program, the principal hopes to hire a trainer to conduct an in-service workshop for educators to better align their teaching with the math textbooks.

St. Felipe's annually administers the Stanford Nine Assessment (SAT-9) in all grades. The principal acknowledges that student scores are very low—in the second stanine in math and in the third in reading. She admits to be perplexed by the low scores, because, as she underscores, the children are very bright. They have the capacity to memorize rap lyrics and enormous detail about sports figures, she says, but can't seem to memorize spelling words, vocabulary, or math times tables. Thus, the challenge, she believes, is for teachers to develop techniques to reach the children. She is convinced children can do better at learning if only they are properly motivated.

Like St. Felipe's, St. Milton's also administers the SAT-9 every year to all students. There is some sentiment among the faculty that the timing of this is unfair to children. Administering it so soon after the summer vacation, children may not yet be re-accustomed to academic thinking. Furthermore, it is frequently very hot in September, making concentration difficult. Students reported that when the scores were released a bulletin from the school told parents that scores were low due to the reasons just described. Teachers in the middle and upper grades report paying particularly close attention to test results and placing greater emphasis in their teaching on subjects and skills for which the SAT-9 showed their school grade to have large numbers of students below average. The first-grade teacher, however, feels that standardized testing is inappropriate for children at this grade. She made it quite clear she regrets being required to administer the Stanford test.

Perhaps the most salient difference between the curricular programs of Christian schools and public establishments is the daily 45-minute period allotted to catechism and religious instruction. But, as already described in Chapter 3, a lower-grade teacher at St. Donat's confessed to us that, when she finds herself under pressure, she sometimes may cut the catechism period to emphasize reading or math. At St. Jeremy's Lutheran School, on the other hand, school administrators and educators have adopted a strategy of closer integration between religious objectives and state curricular guidelines. Every subject of the academic program is organized around religious themes. As the school's principal explained, "kids are going to learn songs, they're going to do essays, they're going to do research papers." They will do these things by learning church songs, writing poems about their faith, and doing research papers "from a religious perspective." The school, as the principal noted proudly, "has promoted outcome-based education . . . for 85 years. We want children to accept the Lord Jesus as their savior. And that's an outcome. We very much are interested in the outcome."

These same themes are echoed in other religious schools. At Shalom Ieladim, for instance, religious education is a central aspect of its raison d'être, as well as a key consideration for parents who enroll their children here, rather than in the high-quality public academic schools in its local district. The school academic program complements a rigorous general studies curriculum with Judaic and Hebrew studies. Religious instruction and related activities demand about 40 percent of students' time.

The demands of this two-tiered curriculum on children, especially the youngest ones, are great. But, in spite of the reduced time dedicated to the standard curriculum, a first-grade teacher remarks that "even though I'm only teaching 60 percent of the time for the general studies program, I think I still try to cram in 100 percent general studies education. I don't want the children to be missing anything." The general studies curriculum at Shalom Ieladim, teachers underscore, follows the state academic framework closely.

Within the boundaries laid out by the state academic frameworks, teachers enjoy significant discretion to design their lesson plans and academic program. As the principal explains,

> When I hire a teacher, I feel this is someone who can bring something really good to the school. And they need the opportunity of doing it. Sort of like "academic freedom." We do follow frameworks on each grade but there's a lot of latitude so that teachers use their own expertise and creativity to enhance the curriculum. Examples would be, say, our second-grade teacher. She is a science [resource specialist], so her children get an enriched regular program with extra science experiences. . . . The third-grade teacher loves poetry and movement. So the children get an enriched regular curriculum with a little more of an artistic flair to it. . . . I feel very strongly in empowering teachers to use their creativity because I feel the children benefit. I've seen what happens when the third graders go to fourth grade and have to do poetry. How simple it is for them. How comfortable they are and how they can express themselves in so many different ways. It's allowing the teachers to do their thing. I hire them because I think they're the best there is around and you need to give them that freedom.

Teachers command the educational leadership in their classrooms. There is a deep-seated commitment to education among the staff, and a tight collegial environment allows for unrestrained communication and honest exchanges. Teachers usually consult with each other and coordinate their curricula so that, as students progress from grade to grade, they arrive ready to face the scholastic challenges for their academic level. These exchanges of information may happen in formal settings, but most frequently they are the product of informal communications among instructors. Although instructors currently make great efforts to incorporate feedback from other teachers, the administration, or even parents into their lesson plans, the classroom curriculum is largely under their direct jurisdiction and control: "Maybe what's different about this school since it's a small private school is that [we can make] our own decisions. We could do, if we wanted, anything. Of course, we wouldn't feel right without talking it over with each other. Maybe with [the grade teachers below] to see what students might know. . . . Or I'll talk it over with [the principal] if it's something that we think he would have some good suggestions for."

Shalom Ieladim, however, will soon enter into a new phase. As part of its school development plan, the school will seek to become an officially accredited institution. As part of the accreditation process, Shalom Ieladim will have to introduce standardized testing in grades 3, 4, and 5. This policy has been received with trepidation among many teachers on staff who fear that it may alter current school practices. The opposition to standardized testing stems from a concern that it "will change our curriculum and the way we teach." The following remarks attest these sentiments:

> *Lower-grade teacher.* I'm hoping that whatever is on a standardized test really is in line with a lot of the stuff that we are already doing in the class so that it doesn't mean that I really have to change a lot about what I'm doing, but maybe the focus shifts lightly. I'm also hoping that if we take the test at a certain time of the year and we haven't covered certain things because the test is before that, that I'm not expected to somehow make sure they already know everything before the test. . . . We're still trying to figure out exactly what that means. And I have some concerns about it, but I also hope that the way it can happen will work. I have mixed feelings about it.
> *Upper-grade teacher.* The children are used to having an openness and finding solutions to problems in their own time and in their own way. The way we present problems, there'll be three or four different solutions. And they're going to find before them now tests where there is only one right answer and, if they don't know it, they only have 3 seconds to figure it out.

There are teachers who are worried that simply taking the test without preparing them, or with preparing them, is going to change the mind-set of the school to some degree.

Instructors consider the accreditation process to be imposed from outside, principally "driven by the parents." Certification entails high costs, but it provides little value added to the work of teachers themselves. In the eyes of teachers, official legitimation will come at an elevated price.

> The board has decided that [accreditation] is something important to do. It then means that, I think, some of the control of what we do in the class goes out of our hands. We have certain requirements that we have to fulfill. And then there's standardized testing that needs to be done. We haven't had to do [it yet], but now it's going to be required in grades 3 through 5 and that, I think, imposes some restrictions on what we can teach. And it really is going to affect how we teach in some ways. That's something that's been imposed on us . . . especially from the parent community.

Dr. Haim, the principal, makes more explicit how teachers consider that standardized testing may change irrevocably the school's approach to teaching and learning:

> The teachers spent a lot of time on developing different assessment tools for children. They take classroom tests, but they also have children write and keep journals. And they assess their painting and their writing and the things they produce. So there is that form of accountability that teachers feel would be minimized if we give tests. Like the tests would end up the primary thing that's looked at in terms of the child's growth. And parents wouldn't be interested in what kind of writing the child has done, you know, because it didn't show up on the test.

The governing bodies of Shalom Ieladim, however, minimize the effect that standardized testing will bear on the school. A member of the board, for example, exclaims that "if [testing had any kind of impact on teaching practices], I would shoot everyone. There's no reason to." It is further implied that packaged tests may actually aid teachers. "The teachers who are so scared of these things, it could be a genuinely useful tool. If a kid reads a paragraph and can't answer simple questions, then you find out that, oh, it's the mother who's answering the questions at night. How can a teacher know sometimes how much help the kid is getting with homework. Really good teachers could. But there's some gray areas. What can a kid really do?"

The principal adopts the stance that standardized tests are a fact of life, and it is useful for children to learn the skills necessary to do well. Dr. Haim retells the story of a student who took a private middle school entrance exam and left many questions unanswered because "it wasn't right to guess." Testing skills are important skills that will assist children to progress.

Overall, school administrators seem convinced that students will indeed perform well in these examinations, even without any reforms to the current school curricula or pedagogical approaches. These are bright and motivated children that have nothing to fear from normed tests. On the other hand, teachers take an opposite view. They maintain that the introduction of this type of evaluation will damage the classroom environment because it denotes assessing teaching and learning with a tool that is perceived as flawed. While the school governing bodies affirm that everything will be all right, the teaching staff contends that Shalom Ieladim must be prepared to deal with the consequences of these actions.

BUREAUCRACY FOR ALL . . . OR MAYBE FOR NONE

Public school behavior has been portrayed as bounded by bureaucratic mandates. Certainly, there are rules to abide by, lesson plans to submit, curricular frameworks to follow, or standardized tests to show progress in. Yet, at the same time, most teachers enjoy a large degree of autonomy in their classrooms. Public school instructors demonstrate substantial flexibility in responding and adapting to educational mandates, adopting new pedagogical approaches, or experimenting with an amalgam of district-sponsored methodologies and their perceptions of what works best to enhance student learning.

Perhaps, more importantly, teachers emphasized that it is not the official demands or the bureaucratic requirements that ultimately guide their actions. It is a personal and internalized sense of professional responsibility that reaches far beyond a school's formal rules and regulations. The principal at Tatuna Point describes her staff behavior in these terms:

> If we were to draw a broad stereotype, teachers tend to be of a personality type that wants to follow the rules, wants to do well, wants to behave, wants to do what's expected. . . . The accountability structure here is very often self-imposed by the teachers. They want it in on time because they're supposed to get it in on time. They want to do well for the kids. They're here because they care about education. You're probably familiar with studies where they asked teachers why they went into teaching. Overwhelmingly teachers report it's because they want to help, they want to make a difference. . . . So their accountability to what they're doing with their children, I think, relates to their deep beliefs about why they're there and how they can help and what kids need. . . . For instance, they know they have to let me do a formal interview, and they have to come in and have this conference with me. Most of them welcome it. They want to know how they're doing. I really think the biggest accountability is self-imposed in a group of teachers. All these other things are there. If they don't turn in x, y, or z in a reasonable time, I might pop a note in their box, "Did you forget x, y, or z?" But there's a big self-imposition. That's why they're here so late. There's no such thing as 9 to 3. That's a rare, rare, rare teacher who goes home right at the end of the day. And there's no one telling them they have to have these four lessons planned or this many things to hand out or cut out those many things. They impose that on themselves. And I think that's a piece that the newspapers miss—the personal dedication that these people feel.

The experience of the private schools that we observed does not deviate significantly from that of their public counterparts. Public and private schools share similar formal administrative and classroom organization. Administrative staff and teachers attend to comparable duties and espouse similar educational goals: principals tend to management issues and oversee the overall functioning of the school, while instructors are mainly responsible for pedagogical classroom concerns. In both public and private schools, teachers report to the principal, while principals are accountable to a super-ordinate body—district officers in the case of public organizations, church officials in parochial schools and a board of directors in private independent schools.

We found no clear distinctions between public and private schools in how they approached teacher personnel issues either. Although Christian schools considered a candidate's religious affiliation as an important qualification, all schools found their selection constricted by a statewide teacher shortage. Peer selection procedures were common in both public and private schools. This approach seemed to assure the selection of teachers whose pedagogical skills were consistent with school themes.

In most cases, the teacher formal evaluation system was not very meaningful or useful. However, most teachers welcomed the informal advice of their principal regarding their teaching styles and effectiveness. Team-teaching schemes and peer collaborative efforts were featured in several public and private schools. Schools did not differ significantly either on their dismissal procedures. Private and public schools showed equal reticence to fire teachers in fear of the potential for litigation. The process for terminating teachers could be nearly as cumbersome and bureaucratic in private as in public schools.

In some instances, the bureaucratic burden on principals and teachers could be described as alike in public and private schools. Church bureaucratic rules and control, most saliently, can be just as onerous or laissez-faire as district or state bureaucracy, largely depending on the parish and archdiocese. The principal at St. Donat's described the barrage of bureaucratic demands she encounters in following way:

> We have what we call the archdiocesan regulations and guidelines. Every principal has administrative handbooks. And then there are curriculum

guidelines that are always current. We look at the guidelines carefully, but we do have the freedom to adapt those guidelines according to the needs of the students. . . . There are certain textbook sets we're given. . . . And they have come out with technology guidelines for the school. . . . The archdiocese recently came up with a new policy for financial policies also, for both parishes and schools. We have to adhere to those very strictly. . . . They have deadlines for different reports that you have to hand in dealing with the federal government. . . . They really keep close tabs so they know exactly who hands in what and at what time. At the beginning of the year, it's a very pressured time, especially September, October when you're having to get all these reports in. No one is exempt from that. . . . We have a survey of school population, finances, staffing, how many credentialed teachers there are, salaries, years of teaching, etc. And a budget statement from the previous year, how much and what we are projecting for this year. It's pretty comprehensive. And then they're very interested to know what the ethnic makeup of your school is.

I believe that [bureaucratic demands] reflect general legalistic demands on all schools, no one's exempt. Whether you're in the public sector or in the private sector, you've got to be prepared. You've got to follow these regulations to protect yourself. It's harder now. When I first started out, none of this existed. I can see there's a lot that's good, but still it does take a lot of time. Sometimes I really get very annoyed because I want to spend more time in the area of curriculum or staff development and working with teachers. And, literally, I walked in here the first month of school and I had to do those reports. I get real resentful toward that because that's a very important part of the year. It's when the new children, the students come in. Some teachers are new and they also need your support. But this has to be done.

Educators in the private and public sectors largely follow similar curricular frameworks, attend similar professional development workshops, fulfill similar professional evaluation procedures, and monitor student progress (and align their lesson plans) with similar standardized tests. But in *both* private and public schools, curricular controls tend to be loose rather than tight. We found no evidence that teachers in public schools necessarily had less freedom in the classroom than private school teachers.

For example, a teacher at St. Felipe's recounts that, officially, the faculty handbook states that the principal must review teacher lesson plans regularly. Yet, because the handbook directions allow for the principal to receive these plans after lessons have actually occurred, there is little in this monthly routine that provides any evidence of what actually happens in class. "I can be lying in the plan book, giving [the principal] one plan and doing the opposite."

A public school teacher echoes this criticism in a statement about the ritual character of curricular planning: "We must turn in the lesson plans to the principal. They often say the reason behind it is in case of an emergency, but none of us writes lesson plans that are detailed enough that a sub could actually follow them. . . . To do a week's worth [of lesson plans] at a time is really just a big deal for me. So a lot of us are really bad at doing them."

Personal discretion and adaptability are a dominant feature of classroom teaching in public and private institutions alike. When bureaucratic regulations are perceived to offer little value added, public and private school teachers often choose to disregard or sidestep such directives. During our classroom observations, we saw many attempts to develop new and more creative curricular approaches. This was true in both public and private schools. But in other schools, both public and private, we also observed un-inspired teaching that was simply textbook driven. In an urban religious school, for instance, students were using an antiquated edition of a science textbook. In several of the public and private low-income schools that we observed, the teachers' favored method of instruction was to ask students consecutively to stand, read a paragraph aloud from the textbook, and then sit down.

From 2 years of classroom observations in the public and private schools of our sample, many examples of creative teaching also come easily to mind. A seventh-grade teacher at Mashita used the soundtrack from *The Phantom of the Opera* to apply the concepts of metaphor and simile. She paused after each verse to analyze the poetry. A fourth-grade instructor at Olympic taught a lesson on probability by describing the variety of colored socks she had at home in her sock drawer. She then asked students to figure out which socks she was likely to wear to school the next day if she picked them when blindfolded. A social studies teacher at Shalom Ieladim attempted to bring the experience of apartheid in South Africa closer to home by engaging students in a classroom play.

Many analysts have claimed that private schools are more willing and able than public schools to organize themselves for high academic achievement, through more flexible curricula, more responsive teacher hiring and firing policies, and more stringent teacher evaluation procedures. Private schools have been portrayed as having a great deal more discretion in terms of choosing what they do and how they do it. We found no evidence of such systematic differences. The public–private dichotomy was not an instructive theory for understanding how schools organize themselves to deliver higher academic achievement. Indeed, there can be great variation in the delivery of schooling services. But these differences can exist within schools as well as across schools in the public and private sectors. Our observations, instead, point toward a different answer. Academic rigidity and lack of innovation appear to stem from another root cause. Where school leaders and teachers are less trained and less skilled, they are less likely to be able to deviate from the mechanics of official mandates and the formal curriculum.

[5]

HOW DIFFERENT ARE PUBLIC SCHOOLS FROM PRIVATE?

Many analysts have claimed that private schools are more willing and able than public schools to respond to parents and to organize themselves for high academic achievement through more flexible curricula and teacher hiring and firing policies. Such claims appear plausible and acceptable in an America that is much less sympathetic to government-run activities than it was thirty years ago. Although a high percentage of Americans are still committed to public education, particularly public schooling for their own children, arguments that the public *system* has serious problems are widely accepted as true. When the criticism focuses on inner-city schools run by large school district administrations, public system failure and the organizational effectiveness of private alternatives are especially believable.

We question these claims. One reason to be skeptical is the lack of evidence that students from similar social backgrounds actually make greater achievement gains in private schools. Studies showing greater gains are mainly limited to Catholic secondary schools (Coleman, Hoffer, and Kilgore, 1982; Bryk, Lee, and Holland,

1993), although some voucher studies following small numbers of African-American students also find that they do better in private primary schools (Howell et al., 2000; Mayer et al., 2002). When studies do report greater achievement gains for private school students, the differences are small.

But even if empirical studies fail to show consistently larger academic gains for students in private schools, many analysts continue to argue that there is an organizational logic to the academic superiority of private education. This logic maintains that private schools are more responsive to parents and more innovative and flexible to organize for high achievement. It argues that market discipline (Friedman, 1955; Jencks, 1966; Chubb and Moe, 1990) and/or communitarian (religious) culture (Jencks, 1966; Coleman and Hoffer, 1987; Bryk, Lee, and Holland, 1993) is bound to produce better education than public schools.

Such differences should be observable in schools through classroom visits and interviews with parents, teachers, and staff. We went to sixteen schools in California to do just that. We wanted to discover how private schools did a better job than public in delivering academic achievement and whether this squared with what analysts claimed. Yet we were unable to find evidence of systematic differences.

Our study was not a random survey, and it was limited to a relatively small number of schools. Whatever lessons we draw in comparing types of schools must be qualified by these limitations. We have tried to be careful in drawing a variety of impressions to show that there is considerable variation among schools, both private and public. Given the restrictions of a small sample of sixteen schools, we did our best to ensure that the schools that we chose represented a typical range of different kinds of public and private schools. Such a sample can at least give us clues about how private and public schools may differ and how they may not.

ARE PRIVATE SCHOOLS BETTER ORGANIZED FOR ACADEMIC ACHIEVEMENT?

The argument for the greater organizational efficiency of privately managed education depends on two main assertions. One is that when parents are allowed to choose among schools competing in an education market administrators and teachers are forced to be more responsive. This makes them more efficient in meeting parent demands than monopoly public schools. The second is that private schools have a great deal more discretion in terms of choosing what they do and how they do it. They are less conflictive because of greater homogeneity of interests among parents and teachers, and administrators are not diverted from their academic mission by hierarchical (public) bureaucracies.

Our case studies suggest that these claims would be difficult to sustain in any careful comparison of private and public schools. We did find that private schools consciously tend to compete for students. Public schools are much less likely to do so. Public school enrollment is usually a function of demographics and the requirements of providing education to children wherever they are. We observed private schools that drew students away from public schools because they offered an educational package that differed from the public package in that school district. But we found that many private schools do not compete with public schools by offering higher academic achievement. Instead, most offer religious education and, as important, the moral and disciplinary environment associated with it. Parents placing a high value on a religious educational environment or on the greater safety and discipline that it promises tend to send their children to religious schools. Obviously, religious education would not be an option for public schools, but a highly disciplined environment that included uniforms and tough behavior codes could be.

Other private schools, usually those competing for students from higher-educated, higher-income families (since they charge high tuition), may offer a particular method of teaching, special language programs; strong discipline (e.g., military academies);

small class sizes; a focus on computers, math, and science; or just plain exclusivity. Some private schools are able to fill these niche markets based mainly on their purported academic excellence (as do some public magnet schools). But many if not most private schools do not focus on academics in distinguishing themselves from public schools. Indeed, academic programs in the vast majority of private schools tend to be no more or less innovative than those in public schools, despite the greater flexibility that private schools may have in providing different curricula or teaching methods. As Brown (1992) has argued, most parents are not risk takers when it comes to their children's education. So private schools competing for students are not likely to offer anything but tried-and-true approaches to teaching and learning and focus instead on nonacademic features that distinguish them from public education.

Our study suggested something else to us about the way that schools operate. We learned that, among schools focusing on academic excellence, private schools do have at their disposal a much greater possibility than their public counterparts of ridding themselves of students and teachers who do not fit in well with their mission. But we found that private schools are more likely to use this option in pushing out students (and their families) than in firing teachers. And when teachers are made to leave, it is usually an outcome of grossly inappropriate behavior, persistent parental pressure, or lack of fit with the nonacademic part of private schools' programs, such as religious teachings. This is logical and increasingly so. First, fear of litigation acts as a deterrent for staff dismissals. Second, as class size reduction efforts in public schools get implemented, overall teacher shortages increase and public school salaries rise. In this environment, private schools also must come to grips with teacher shortages. Firing teachers is less an option when it is difficult to replace them. For many private schools, even those focused on academic achievement, easing out troublesome parents and students may be a lower cost option than replacing middling teachers.

We also discovered that Chubb and Moe's description of public schools as being riddled with competing interests, unable to find academic focus, and brought to a lowest common denominator by an overarching, rigid bureaucracy is inaccurate. So is, we found, their conception of private schools as having a clear purpose, little conflict, and innovative, flexible administrations. Many private schools in our sample were as much or more characterized by profound conflicts than public schools. The locus of conflict was usually nonacademic. Religious schools are particularly susceptible to conflicts over the religious–academic mix or, in one case, what the content of religious education should be. Such issues are deeply divisive. The bilingual immersion school in our sample had different groups of parents representing different language groups trying to push the school in different directions. Public schools are also conflictive places. The conflicts are more likely to be academic in high-income communities and related to safety and behavioral problems in low-income communities. But the ways that the conflicts are settled in private and public schools tend to be different. We observed that private schools are more likely to define clear boundaries and stick to a course that the school head and/or the majority on the school's governing body deems best for the school, sometimes at the cost of shedding dissidents. Public schools do not have this option. They must live with dissent, often making changes first in one direction and then another.

Parent participation in this variety of conditions differs, but not in the way we expected. Both public *and* private schools serving lower-income populations have difficulty getting parents to be active in school activities. Many private schools in this category try to resolve the problem by requiring parents either to volunteer for certain tasks or contribute cash to buy themselves out of their time commitment. They also often make parents sign contracts concerning responsibility for their children's behavior and academic work as a condition of enrolling their child in the school. Public schools cannot make such demands (although charter schools have gained some leeway to mandate parental participation in support of their children's education). Public schooling is a right, not a privilege. Public school teachers and administrators do try to get lower-income parents involved, but mainly through direct teacher and administrator contact and, more rarely, through schoolwide efforts that focus on school–community relations.

We found that, whether schools are public or private or enroll children from lower- or higher-income families, teachers and administrators do not encourage parents to tell them what or how to teach. Rather, school personnel want parents to participate in academic activities by being supportive, particularly in getting their children to work hard academically and conform to school rules. Parents choose to send their children to a particular private school and pay to do so. At least initially, they agree with and accept the educational package offered. But in the private schools that we observed we found that efforts to influence the package were generally not welcomed. The longer the waiting list for the private school, the more school personnel can place demands on parents to align themselves with school conceptions of a good education. In effect, private schools generally define what they are offering to parents; parents who like that package enroll their children and participate in school activities by donating time or money and supporting school demands on their children. Active parent participation aimed at influencing academic or core nonacademic activities occurred in many of the private schools in our sample, but these dissident parents and their children were usually encouraged to go elsewhere. True, if this happens repeatedly, the school will face difficulties. Yet, in all the cases we observed, the schools quickly found new students to replace those who had left.

Thus, the responsiveness to parents that analysts refer to in discussing private schools has much more to do with what Hirschman (1970) called "exit" than what he called "voice." Schools are "responsive" to parents by creating a package of services that enough parents want so that the school fills its seats. But, once enrolled, private schools are not necessarily receptive to parental demands. Parents who come into conflict with private schools may be steered to leave (exit), rather than exert influence through voice.

Public schools have a much harder time getting rid of dissident parents or stifling dissent. Parents often press public schools on nonacademic issues (school safety or sports, for example). But we observed that in high-income neighborhoods, high test scores, advanced placement courses, college entrance, or the way that math and science are taught are the objects of intense scrutiny and active "voice" by parents. The bottom line is that public schools are objects of *public* discussion and hence subject to public pressures. We found that, in the face of parental demands, public schools have little choice, but, in the least, they make a perfunctory effort to address parental concerns and strive to accommodate their requests.

WHAT DOES THE STUDY TELL US ABOUT EDUCATIONAL POLICY?

Proponents of increasing the private role in American education contend that education would improve significantly if private schooling were allowed to expand. Improvement would be especially great, they argue, for low-income students now attending public schools in urban centers. Most proposals for expanding private education have centered on providing vouchers that could be used in any school, public or private. More recently, however, charter laws in some states, such as Arizona and Ohio, have allowed private schools to apply for charter status and thus get access to public funds. In addition, private management companies, such as Edison, operate public schools for profit.

The promotion of expanded private schooling as a solution to America's education problems has come from many sources. Milton Friedman (1955) made the case in terms of the free market versus government provision of services. Then, in the late 1960s, liberal academics at Harvard pushed for expanded private and nonprivate educational competition as a government-regulated market alternative to bureaucratized urban public school monopolies (Jencks, 1966; Center for the Study of Public Policy, 1970). Later, in the 1980s, the focus was on the advantages of expanding Catholic education as a communitarian alternative to public bureaucracy for urban minority youth. Now, the free-market proponents have returned in force, but they focus heavily on urban minority youth while sponsoring statewide initiatives for more generalized voucher plans.

The policy discussion around expanding private education varies among analysts, depending on what they see it achieving. We can divide the discussion into three main branches.

1. Proponents all make the case for subsidizing private education in terms of expanding educational choice and the benefits that greater choice would provide. Most analysts have argued that choice is especially restricted for low-income families, so expanding private education alternatives for the poor would be particularly beneficial. The main benefit of choice is simply that families feel better off when they can choose. But choice also benefits those families who prefer educational packages not provided by typical public schools. The most evident of these is greater emphasis on religion and morality. The major policy issue here is whether the greater benefits associated with subsidizing private religious schools conflicts with fundamental principles of secular politics. Proponents argue that benefits far outweigh any political costs. Civil libertarians oppose subsidizing religious schools. They argue that these benefits can be generated for most families by allowing greater choice among public schools offering different types of programs, whether within districts, across districts, or within district autonomous charter schools.

2. Proponents also directly or implicitly argue that private schools are more efficient in delivering academic skills than public schools. Friedman contends that private schools can provide the same academic skills for lower cost; other analysts claim that

private schools are both cheaper (Catholic schools) and produce higher achievement than for similar students in public schools. The reasons given for this greater efficiency focus mainly on the role of market competition in making institutions, such as schools, more conscious of consumer wants and hence more likely to organize themselves for producing the greatest possible amount of student achievement. Since private schools have to compete for students, they focus more on achievement than bureaucratized public monopolies that are guaranteed their students every year. From a policy standpoint, competition could occur among public schools through choice programs; but proponents argue that market discipline would prevail only when private schools, which depend entirely on competition for students, would be allowed to enter the fray.

3. Others have argued that religious schools may be more effective academically less because of market discipline and more because their teaching philosophy is rooted in communitarian religious values. These promote a sense of belonging and security, especially important for students coming from low-income families, and this, in turn, motivates them to learn. If this were the only argument for the greater effectiveness of private education—and that mainly for low-income students—the most important policy implication might not be the expansion of private religious education, but rather a greater emphasis on communitarian values in public education. This would include smaller schools, higher expectations, tighter student–teacher bonds, and more emphasis on moral education and uniforms (to promote school identification). Bryk, Lee, and Holland (1993) came to the conclusion that public schools could incorporate many of these features of Catholic secondary schools.

Our study of private and public schools cannot speak to all these policy issues. We had a limited agenda of trying to understand whether private and public elementary and middle schools differ in the way that they are organized to deliver academic achievement.

We can say little about the total benefits of greater choice for families who have choice versus those who don't. The parents we interviewed at private schools were not universally satisfied with their schools, nor were parents with children in public schools. Yet making the case for choice is easy in a society that places such a high value on it. Policies that expand educational choice without reducing local public school revenue or forcing voters to confront political values such as the separation of church and state would certainly be widely accepted. Public opinion polls suggest that those groups who feel poorly served by the public system may even support a choice system that reduces the tax dollars going to pub- lic schools and diverts them to religious education (Bositis, 1999).

We had just one opportunity to note the impact on a neighborhood school that competition from another with a unique academic focus can have. Less than 5 miles from Mashita Middle School is another public middle school, Kriz. Kriz is a magnet school with a curriculum built around a "math and science gifted" theme. The Mashita school principal, Ms. Sajon, estimates that, were it not for Kriz, Mashita would be able to enroll a more affluent student body. She does not attribute the draw of the magnet school solely to its academic focus. She believes that parents are influenced by the fact that Kriz Magnet is a new, attractive facility in a wealthy residential neighborhood in a separately incorporated suburban community, while Mashita has old-fashioned architecture and is closer to a major, run-down commercial thoroughfare. But Ms. Sajon believes that, whatever the reason for the attraction, if parents are concerned enough about their children's education to choose a magnet school, this indicates that these parents would be those who, had they remained at their neighborhood school, would have been more involved than the typical parent in school booster activities and other forms of involvement.

School choice theorists suggest that competition from Kriz Magnet should force Mashita to respond by improving its academic outcomes or other attractive features in order to discourage neighborhood families from choosing to send their children to Kriz. Consistent with what this approach would predict, Mashita is currently remodeling a performing arts center on its campus because, Ms. Sajon states, "we see that as a major draw." In addition, the faculty has voted to become part of a major reform program of the school district primarily because this would permit Mashita to apply for major foundation grants. Mashita, together with other schools in its high school cluster, then applied for a technology grant. Mashita has become the pilot demonstration school for the cluster. Ms. Sajon believes that this technology center will also help to attract families who have other choices.

On the other hand, choice theory also suggests the "creaming" effect about which Ms. Sajon is concerned: if the most educationally motivated middle-class families in the community choose to send their children to Kriz, Mashita then loses the parental involvement of those families who would most likely be a force in the school community for higher standards and teacher accountability and would most likely be a source of volunteer time or additional resources. Mashita is buffeted by both of these countervailing forces—competition to improve and loss of the most highly motivated parents and children—emanating from the presence of the nearby magnet school. In summary, as this case study attests, competition can bring about some healthy consequences, yet it also comes hand in hand with some very deleterious ones.

We can say much more from our study about policies that aim to expand private education, religious or otherwise, to improve student achievement. We are convinced that there is little evidence to support such policies. We draw our conclusions mostly from reviewing the empirical studies comparing student achievement gains in public and private schools. More recently, proponents of private education expansion have been trying to show that competition from private or charter schools improves achievement in public schools. But such studies are not very persuasive either (see Carnoy, 2001).

Our observations in schools also suggest strongly that shifting public funding to private schools would not result in higher achievement levels. We could not find anything particularly unusual or innovative about the way that private school teachers teach academic subjects. From what we saw and heard in terms of service delivery, it was practically impossible to distinguish between private and public schools without prior knowledge of their funding or obvious religious imagery. Private schools had one important advantage: They could shed disruptive or difficult students. If this weren't the case, private school teachers would probably face many of the same difficulties as public school teachers, and they would be about as likely to deal with them effectively.

In other words, we could observe the alleged influence of market discipline on the provision of a greater variety of school types, such as religious schools or language immersion schools, than in the public sector. But we could not observe any special organizational logic in private schools that would make them better at producing higher achievement than public schools with similar students. Until researchers come up with persuasive evidence that the market produces more than just greater variety in educational packages offered by schools, policymakers should reject claims for private education producing higher achievement.

Bryk, Lee, and Holland's conclusion that public schools could incorporate many of the communitarian features that help Catholic schools to be more successful with inner-city youth (according to Coleman and Hoffer, 1987, and Bryk, Lee and Holland, 1993) leads to another policy question. What can public schools learn from private ones to improve public education?

The usual answer to this question is that public schools should become more like private schools in responding to parent demands, in focusing on academic achievement, and in hiring good teachers and firing bad ones. But we found that private schools were much like public schools in all these areas. Our study therefore points away from the arguments that public schools need to adopt the greater accountability to parents and the flexibility in hiring and firing teachers characteristic of private schools. These may be good policies for all schools to follow, but public schools with students from upper-middle-class families are just as likely to be accountable to their parents as private schools serving the same clientele. Similarly, we found no evidence that private schools evaluated teachers more often or with greater stringency than public schools.

The private (and public charter) schools that we observed that offered a unique academic approach (like dual-language immersion or a constructivist pedagogy) tended to cater to both relatively affluent and/or highly educated parents. These schools clearly met a need that neighborhood public schools did not fulfill.

But public schools that are poorly run can learn their most important lessons from well-run public *and* private schools. And we have uncovered no evidence that these lessons will be diffused through increased market accountability. We suspect there may be two reasons for this. First, private schools do not appear to be inherently more effective than public; hence more private schools in an education market will not necessarily mean more good models. Second, although some private (and public choice) schools have unique academic programs, many private schools appear to compete for students mainly by offering nonacademic products (religion, safety, or a unique environment) that differentiate them from their public counterparts in the same market. So the lesson that might be learned is how to differentiate a product mix, rather than deliver more academic learning.

We need to note some differences between our observations and conclusions and those of a highly regarded comparison of

Catholic and public schools, Bryk, Lee, and Holland's *Catholic Schools and the Common Good* (1993). In some respects, of course, our work is not comparable. Bryk, Lee, and Holland's study was of secondary schools, whereas this report concerns only elementary schools. Their fieldwork took place in "good" Catholic high schools, whereas we, while not excluding schools of exceptional quality, made no effort to select schools on this basis.

Like Bryk and his colleagues, we also found Catholic school faculties with an educational philosophy that went beyond academic concerns to issues of social justice and moral behavior. But we found such sense of purpose also in some public schools that we observed and in some non-Catholic private schools as well. Bryk, Lee, and Holland's description of schools "organized around strong normative principles," combining a "strong emphasis on academic work with a caring ethos that demands personal responsibility," with a set of "humanistic beliefs and social principles" (p. 327) characterized, to some extent, the Catholic elementary schools that we observed, but could equally characterize the faculties of United and Renaissance public schools, or could describe some administrators and teachers at Madison and Olympic charters, or could also portray the leaders of non-Catholic private schools like Shalom Ieladim.

Our primary difference with Bryk and his colleagues, however, stems from their observation that parents in Catholic schools, to a greater extent than in other schools, participate in a "voluntary community" where they "ease the work of the school staff by ensuring that students attend regularly, do their homework, and adhere to the school's behavioral standards" and that their relationship to school staffs can be characterized as a "trust relationship" (pp. 305–6). There were certainly parents with whom we spoke, and about whom the faculty we interviewed spoke, for whom such characterizations applied. But we did not observe these to be particularly more frequent in private or in Catholic schools as a whole. Rather, in this respect as in so many others, the social, cultural, and economic backgrounds of the parents and the community in which the school was located seemed to be the main determinant of variation, much more so than a school's public or private character or, within the latter group, whether it was religious or secular. Within particular communities, the similarities between schools and the problems that they confronted overwhelmed the differences.

Thus, the main division we found in the schools that we visited was not between sectors—private versus public—but between schools, both private and public, serving different socioeconomic communities. The personnel in a private elementary school in a low-income community teach children and deal with parents much like the teachers and staff of a public school in the same community. Likewise, it is difficult to distinguish a private school classroom from a public in a high-income suburb. But there are major differences in what is taught in private or public schools in high- and low-income neighborhoods. Both private and public schools serving low-income families find it difficult to get parents to participate. Both private and public schools serving high-income families have to control overzealous parents.

Jean Anyon (1983) was mostly right in showing that schools serving different social-class groups teach different academic skills, not only because school personnel have different expectations of children from lower-income families than of children from higher-income families, but because parents of these children also have different conceptions of a good education. We found that less educated parents living in low-income communities who send their children to private schools don't demand that the schools teach their children a high-powered, problem-solving curriculum. These parents worry more about greater safety and a more disciplined environment for their children. Higher-educated parents living in high-income communities also demand from private education about the same academic curriculum as is taught in suburban public schools, but, in addition, greater exclusivity, smaller class sizes, or specialized programs not offered by public schools.

If the primary division between high- and low-powered academics is not the private and public one, but between schools serving different social-class children, the market–public dichotomy is not irrelevant to policy concerned with raising academic achievement. It implies that simply increasing competition among schools, subsidizing private education, or turning schools over to private management is not going to solve the achievement gap between children from families with less educated parents and those from upper-middle-class households headed by professional adults. Neither will it solve the black–white test score gap.

One major reason that the market solution to social problems is so appealing is that it claims to give so much potential bang for such low cost. Proponents of privatization have stressed that the main costs to be paid by allowing competition to the public monopoly over education would be borne by teachers' unions—not by teachers themselves, who would be liberated from conforming to oppressive bureaucratic regulations—and superfluous administrators and bureaucrats. No doubt that many large urban school districts could be streamlined bureaucratically, and no doubt that teachers' unions could be more creative in fashioning educational improvement. But if the market solution to educational achievement is not really a solution, why not just focus on streamlining the public system or engaging the teachers' unions to come up with ideas to improve urban education? Why make any groups pay high costs for a change that is unlikely to make things better?

The potentially most costly aspect to focusing on the private–public division is that it may persuade the public that improving education is just a problem of reducing inefficient public bureaucracy. If public officials and voters come to believe that we can raise academic skills sharply by just shifting children from publicly to privately run schools, they would conveniently avoid any programs that require long-term investments in teacher and facilities improvements, reducing class size, or early education.

Given what we have learned, it would be difficult to increase academic achievement in low-income neighborhoods without making education there approach the teaching and curriculum that children get in higher-income suburban schools, from early childhood to late adolescence. Policies that avoid this reality may produce educational change, but are unlikely to affect how much children learn.

REFERENCES

Abelmann, Charles, and Richard Elmore, with Johanna Even, Susan Kenyon, and Joanne Marshall (1999). "When Accountability Knocks, Will Anyone Answer?" Philadelphia: University of Pennsylvania, Consortium for Policy Research in Education.

Alexander, K. L., and A. M. Pallas (1982). "Reply to Coleman." *American Sociological Review,* 47 (6): 822–824.

Alexander, K. L., and A. M. Pallas (1983). "Private Schools and Public Policy: New Evidence on Cognitive Achievement in Public and Private Schools." *Sociology of Education,* 56: 170–182.

Alexander, K. L., and Pallas, A. M. (1987). "School Sector and Cognitive Performance: When Is a Little a Little?" In *Comparing Public and Private Schools. Volume 2: School Achievement,* edited by E. H. Haertel, T. James, and H. M. Levin. New York: Falmer Press, pp. 89–111.

American Federation of Teachers (2000). *Trends in Student Achievement for Edison Schools, Inc.: The Emerging Track Record.* Downloaded from: www.aft.org/research/edisonschools/2000edison.pdf

Anyon, Jean (1983). "Social Class and the Hidden Curriculum of Work." *The Hidden Curriculum and Moral Education: Deception or Discovery?* Henry Giroux and David Purpel. Berkeley, CA: McCutchan Publishing Corp. pp. 143–167.

Baker, David P., and Cornelius Riordan (1999a). "The 'Eliting' of the Common American Catholic School and the National Education Crisis." *Phi Delta Kappan,* 80 (1): 16–23.

Baker, David P., and Cornelius Riordan (1999b). "It's Not about the Failure of Catholic Schools: Its about Demographic Transformations." *Phi Delta Kappan,* 80 (6): 462–463, 478.

Bositis, Davis (1999). *1999 National Opinion Poll—Education.* Washington, DC: Joint Center for Political and Economic Studies.

Bositis, David (2001)."School Vouchers along the Color Line," *New York Times,* August 15, p. A27.

Bowles, Samuel, and Henry M. Levin (1968). "The Determinants of Schooling Achievement: An Appraisal of Some Recent Evidence," *Journal of Human Resources,* 3 (1): 3–24.

Brown, Byron (1992). "Why Governments Run Schools." *Economics of Education Review,* 11 (4): 287–300.

Bryk, Anthony S., and Valerie Lee (1992). "Is Politics the Problem and Markets the Answer? An Essay Review of Politics, Markets and America's Schools." *Economics of Education Review,* 11 (4): 439–451.

Bryk, Anthony S., Valerie Lee, and Peter Holland (1993). *Catholic Schools and the Common Good.* Cambridge, MA: Harvard University Press.

Carnoy, Martin (2000). *Sustaining the New Economy: Work, Family, and Community in the Information Age.* Cambridge, MA: Harvard University Press and Russell Sage Foundation.

Carnoy, Martin (2001). *School Vouchers: Examining the Evidence.* Washington, DC: Economic Policy Institute.

Carnoy, Martin, and Henry M. Levin (1985). *Schooling and Work in the Democratic State.* Stanford, CA: Stanford University Press.

Carnoy, Martin, and Derek Shearer (1980). *Economic Democracy.* Armonk, NY: Sharpe.

Catterall, James S. (1988). "Private School Participation and Public School Policy." In *Comparing Public and Private Schools, Vol. 1: Institutions and Organizations,* edited by T. James and H. M. Levin. Philadelphia: Falmer Press, pp. 46–60.

Center for the Study of Public Policy (1970). *Education Vouchers: A Report on Financing Elementary Education by Grants to Parents.* Cambridge, MA: Center for the Study of Public Policy.

Chubb, John, and Terry Moe (1990). *Politics, Markets, and America's Schools.* Washington, DC: Brookings Institution.

Clune, William H., and John F. Witte (eds.) (1990). *Choice and Control in American Education. Volume 1: The Theory of Choice and Control in Education.* New York: Falmer Press.

Cobb, Casey, and Gene Glass (2001). "U.S. Charter Schools and Ethnic Segregation: Inspecting the Evidence." *International Journal of Educational Reform,* 10 (4): 381–395.

Coleman, J. S. (1990). "Choice, Community, and Future Schools," In *Choice and Control in American Education, Volume 1: The Theory of Choice and Control in Education,* edited by W. H. Clune, and J. F. Witte. London: Falmer Press, p. ix.

Coleman, James S., Thomas Hoffer, and Sally Kilgore (1982). *High School Achievement.* New York: Basic Books.

Coleman, James, and Thomas Hoffer (1987). *Public and Private High Schools: The Impact of Communities.* New York: Basic Books.

Coleman, J. S., et al. (1966). *Equality of Educational Opportunity Report.* Washington, DC: U.S. Government Printing Office.

Cookson, Peter (1994). *School Choice: The Struggle for the Soul of American Education.* New Haven, CT: Yale University Press.

Cookson, Peter, and Caroline Hodges Persell (1985). *Preparing for Power.* New York: Basic Books.

Cooper, Bruce E. (1988). "The Changing Universe of U.S. Private Schools," in James, T. and H. M. Levin (eds.), *Comparing Public and Private Schools, Vol. 1: Institutions and Organizations.* Philadelphia: Falmer Press, pp. 18–45.

Dewey, John (1976). *The Middle Works, 1902–1903.* Edited by Jo Ann Boydston. Carbondale, IL: Southern Illinois University Press.

Elmore, Richard (1993). "School Decentralization: Who Gains? Who Loses?" In *Decentralization and School Improvement,* edited by Jane Hannaway and Martin Carnoy. San Francisco: Jossey-Bass, pp. 33–54.

Evans, W. N. and R. M. Schwab (1995). "Finishing High School and Starting College: Do Catholic Schools Make a Difference?" *Quarterly Journal of Economics,* 110: 941–974.

Finn, Chester E. (1990). "Why We Need Choice." In *Choice in Education: Potential and Problems,* edited by W. L. Boyd and H. J. Walberg. Berkeley, CA: McCutchan Publishing Corp., pp. 21–42.

Finn, Chester, Bruno Manno, and Greg Vanourek (1999). *Charter Schools in Action: Renewing Public Education.* Princeton, NJ: Princeton University Press.

Friedman, Milton (1955). "The Role of Government in Education." In *Economics and the Public Interest,* edited by Robert A. Solo. New Brunswick, NJ: Rutgers University Press, pp 123–144.

Goldberger, A. S., and G. G. Cain (1982). "The Causal Analysis of Cognitive Outcomes in the Coleman, Hoffer and Kilgore Report." *Sociology of Education,* 55 (2/3): 103–122.

Greeley, A. M. (1982). *Catholic High Schools and Minority Students.* New Brunswick, NJ: Transaction Books.

Greeley, Andrew (1999a). "The So-Called Failure of Catholic Schools." *Phi Delta Kappan,* 80 (1): 24–25.

Greeley, Andrew (1999b). "More Assertions Not Backed by Data." *Phi Delta Kappan,* 80 (6): 463.

Greene, Jay (2001). "An Evaluation of the Florida A-Plus Accountability and School Choice Program." New York: Manhattan Institute for Policy Research, Center for Civic Innovation.

Greene, Jay P., Paul E. Peterson, and Jiangtao Du (1996). "The Effectiveness of School Choice in Milwaukee: A Secondary Analysis of Data from the Program's Evaluation." Paper prepared for presentation before the Panel on the Political Analysis of Urban School Systems, American Political Science Association, San Francisco, CA, August 30.

Hanushek, Eric, and John Kain (1972). "On the Value of 'Equality of Educational Opportunity' as a Guide to Public Policy." In *On Equality of Educational Opportunity,* edited by Frederick Mosteller and Daniel Moynihan. New York: Random House, pp. 116–145.

Harkavy, Ira (1998). "School–Community–University Partnerships: Effectively Integrating Community Building and Education Reform." Paper presented at the conference on *Connecting Community Building and Education Reform: Effective School, Community, University Partnerships,* Washington, DC, January 8.

Henig, Jeffrey (1996). "The Local Dynamics of Choice: Ethnic Preferences and Institutional Responses." In *Who Chooses? Who Loses? Culture, Institutions, and the Unequal Effects of School Choice,* edited by B. Fuller and R. Elmore. New York: Teachers College Press, pp. 95–117.

Hirschman, Albert (1970). *Exit, Voice and Loyalty: Responses to Decline in Firms, Organizations and States.* Cambridge, MA: Harvard University Press.

Howell, William, et al. (2000). "Test Score Effects of School Vouchers in Dayton, Ohio, New York City, and Washington, D.C.: Evidence From Randomized Field Trials." Paper prepared for the American Political Science Association meeting, September.

Hoxby, Carolyn (2001). "How School Choice Affects the Achievement of Public School Students." Cambridge, MA: Department of Economics, Harvard University.

Jencks, Christopher (1966). "Is the Public School Obsolete?" *Public Interest,* 2, Winter: 18–27.

Jencks, Christopher (1985). "How Much Do High School Students Learn?" *Sociology of Education,* 58: 128–35.

Jepsen, Christopher (2000). "The Private Schooling Market and Its Effects on Student Achievement." Unpublished Ph.D. dissertation, Northwestern University.

Kirkpatrick, David W. (1990). *Choice in Schooling: A Case for Tuition Vouchers.* Chicago: Loyola University Press.

Lee, V., R. Croninger, and J. Smith (1996). "Equity and Choice in Detroit." In *Who Chooses? Who Loses? Culture, Institutions, and the Unequal Effects of School Choice,* edited by B. Fuller and R. Elmore. New York: Teachers College Press, pp. 70–94.

Levin, Henry M. (1998). "Accelerated Schools: A Decade of Evolution." In *International Handbook of Educational Change,* edited by Andy Hargreaves et al. Boston: Kluwer Academic Publishers, pp. 807–830.

Lips, Carrie (2000). "Edupreneurs: A Survey of For-profit Education." *Policy Analysis,* No. 386, November.

Loeb, Susanna, and Marianne Page (1998). "Examining the Link between Wages and Quality in the Teacher Workforce: The Role of Alternative Labor Market Opportunities and Non-Pecuniary Variation," Department of Economics, University of California-Davis (mimeo).

Martinez, V., K. Godwin, and F. Kemerer (1996). "Public School Choice in San Antonio: Who Chooses and with What Effects?" In *Who Chooses? Who Loses? Culture, Institutions, and the Unequal Effects of School Choice,* edited by B. Fuller and R. Elmore. New York: Teachers College Press, pp. 50–69.

Mayer, Daniel, et al. (2002). *School Choice in New York City after Three Years: An Evaluation of the School Choice Scholarships Program.* Princeton, NJ: Mathematica Policy Research, Inc.

McEwan, Patrick, and Martin Carnoy (2000). "The Effectiveness and Efficiency of Private Schools in Chile's Voucher System." *Educational Evaluation and Policy Analysis,* 22 (3 Fall).

Metcalf, Kim (2001). *Cleveland Scholarship Program Evaluation: 1998–2000 Technical Report.* Bloomington, IN: Indiana Center for Evaluation.

Moe, Terry (2001). *A Primer on America's Schools.* Stanford, CA: Hoover Press.

Murnane, Richard J. (1984). "A Review Essay—Comparisons of Public and Private Schools: Lessons from the Uproar." *Journal of Human Resources,* 19: 263–277.

Nathan, Joe (1996). *Charter Schools. Creating Hope and Opportunity for American Education.* San Francisco: Jossey-Bass.

Neal, Derek (1997). "The Effect of Catholic Secondary Schooling on Educational Attainment." *Journal of Labor Economics,* 15: 98–123.

Noell, J. (1982). "Public and Catholic Schools: A Reanalysis of Public and Private Schools." *Journal of Sociology of Education,* 55: 123–132.

Perelman, Lewis (1992). *School's Out.* New York: William Morrow.

Public Policy Forum (2002). "Choice schools enroll fewer KY students." *Research Brief,* vol. 90, no 1, January 23. (Milwaukee, WI).

Ravitch, Diane (1974). *The Great School Wars.* New York: Basic Books.

Rose, Lowell, and Alec Gallup (2001). "The 33rd Annual Phi Delta Kappa/Gallup Poll of the Public's Attitudes toward the Public Schools." *Phi Delta Kappan,* 83 (1): 41–72.

Rouse, Cecilia (1998a). "Private School Vouchers and Student Achievement: Evidence from the Milwaukee Choice Program." *Quarterly Journal of Economics,* 113 (2): 553–602.

Rouse, Cecilia (1998b). "Schools and Student Achievement: More Evidence from the Milwaukee Parental Choice Program." *Federal Reserve Bank of New York Economic Policy Review,* 4 (1): 61–76.

Rumberger, R. (1996). "Dropping out of Middle School: A Multilevel Analysis of Students and Schools." *American Educational Research Journal,* 32 (3): 583–625.

Salganik, L. H., and N. Karweit (1982). "Voluntarism and Governance in Education." *Sociology of Education,* 55: 152–161.

Sander, William (1996). "Catholic Grade Schools and Academic Achievement." *Journal of Human Resources,* 31: 540–548.

Sander, William (2001). "The Effect of Catholic Schools on Religiosity, Achievement and Competition." National Center for the Study of Privatization in Education, Teachers College, Columbia University, Occasional Paper No. 32.

Scott, W. R., and Meyer, J. W. (1988) "Environmental Linkages and Organizational Complexity: Public and Private Schools." In *Comparing Public and Private Schools, Vol. 1: Institutions and Organizations,* edited by T. James and H. M. Levin. Philadelphia: Falmer Press, pp. 128–160.

Talbert, J. E. (1988). "Conditions of Public and Private School Organization and Notions of Effective Schools." In *Comparing Public and Private Schools, Vol. 1: Institutions and Organizations,* edited by T. James and H. M. Levin. Philadelphia: Falmer Press, pp. 161–188.

Thernstrom, Stephan, and Abigail Thernstrom (1998). *America in Black and White.* New York: Simon and Schuster.

Tyack, David (1974). *The One Best System. A History of American Urban Education.* Cambridge, MA: Harvard University Press.

U.S. Department of Education (2001). *Private School Universe Survey: 1999–2000.* Washington, DC: National Center for Education Statistics.

U.S. Department of Education (1999). *Digest of Education Statistics.* Washington, DC: National Center for Education Statistics.

Viadero, Debra (2002). "Voucher Plans' Test Data Yield Puzzling Trends," *Education Week,* 21, 24 (February 27): 5.

Wallis, Claudia (1994). "A Class of Their Own," *Time,* October 31, p. 57.

Wells, Amy Stuart (1999). "California's Charter Schools: Promises vs. Performance." *American Educator,* 23 (1): 18–21, 24, 52.

Williams, Joe (2000). "Choice May Draw 10,000 Students in Fall; 22 New Schools Will Join Voucher Program for Next School Year, DPI Announces." *Milwaukee Journal Sentinel,* May 16.

Willms, J. Douglas (1984). *Public and Private School Outcomes: Results from the High School and Beyond Follow-up Study.* Stanford, CA: Institute for Research on Educational Finance and Governance, School of Education, Stanford University.

Willms, J. Douglas (1987). "Patterns of Academic Achievement in Public and Private Schools: Implications for Public Policy and Future Research." In *Comparing Public and Private Schools. Volume 2: School Achievement,* edited by E. H. Haertel, T. James, and H. M. Levin. New York: Falmer Press, pp. 113–134.

Witte, John F. (1992). "Private School versus Public School Achievement: Are There Findings That Should Affect the Educational Choice Debate?" *Economics of Education Review,* 11: 371–394.

Witte, John (1996). "Who Benefits from the Milwaukee Choice Program." In *Who Chooses? Who Loses? Culture, Institutions and the Unequal Effects of School Choice,* edited by B. Fuller and R. Elmore. New York: Teachers College Press, pp. 118–137.

Witte, John F. (1997). "Reply to Greene, Peterson and Du: 'The Effectiveness of School Choice in Milwaukee: A Secondary Analysis of Data from the Program's Evaluation.'" http://www.harvard.edu/pepg/op/evaluate.htm.

Witte, John F., Troy D. Sterr, and Christopher A. Thorn (1995). "Fifth Year Report: Milwaukee Parental Choice Program." Madison, WI: Department of Political Science and the Robert M. La Follette Center for Public Affairs, University of Wisconsin.

Zunz, Olivier (1982). *The Changing Face of Inequality.* Chicago: University of Chicago Press.

Notes

CHAPTER 1

1. Home schooling confounds these numbers, since there may be about 800,000 to 1 million children in home schooling. Some charter schools are also quasi-private. When children in home schooling and those in quasi-private charter schools are added to the 5.86 million children included in official statistics as private school students in 1997–1998, the private school total may slightly surpass the number attending private school in 1965. However, this is still surprisingly low, given the rise in real family income, particularly since neither the home schooling nor charter schooling alternative requires tuition payments. Furthermore, home schooling is often an alternative for religious reasons, undertaken by lower-income families. Between 1985 and 1999, private school enrollments have grown by approximately 7 percent. In turn, public school enrollments have grown at a faster pace, by around 9 percent (U.S. Department of Education, 1999).

2. Some historians have argued that residential segregation was less meaningful in the early twentieth century because of high social mobility, but Zunz challenges that view.

3. The measures of school success in these studies are high school graduation rates and continuation on to higher education. These measures do not necessarily capture superior academic preparedness or directly imply higher achievement scores by Catholic school students. As Neal (1997) suggests, these findings "do not rule out the possibility that urban students acquire skills at the same rate regardless of whether they attend public or Catholic schools. Public school students may drop out more often for reasons that do not relate directly to the rate of learning in public schools."

4. Catterall reports that only a very small fraction (about 1.5 percent) of black elementary and secondary school students coming from families earning less than $7,500 in 1982 were enrolled in "church-related" private schools (Catterall, 1988, table 7). In 1980, almost 40 percent of black households nationally earned less than $7,500 income. It is safe to say that the sample of low-income black youth attending Catholic secondary schools in 1982 was not representative of low-income black youth.

5. For example, a major discussion in Catholic secondary education at the beginning of the twentieth century was whether to include a vocational track. This was rejected and has since had a major influence on the nature of Catholic high schools.

6. Coleman, Hoffer, and Kilgore (1982) provide an excellent discussion of selection bias (see their Addendum, pp. 199–227). They also use several different methods to correct for bias, showing

that the Catholic school effect remains significant and positive for mathematics achievement even after such corrections.

7. Only 8,000 pupils had taken vouchers by the year 2000. Private schools not in operation when vouchers were offered had to be approved, limiting the supply of new schools. About 90 private schools, 80 percent religious, took voucher students in 2000–2001. During 2001–2002, 107 schools, still mainly religious, accepted voucher students, enrolling another 2,000 children. Even so, the supply of schools to take advantage of a fairly large voucher ($5,500) is slow in materializing. The ten largest choice schools enroll $\frac{1}{3}$ of all voucher students, and nineteen schools enroll half of all voucher students (Public Policy Forum, 2002)

8. Many of the children receiving vouchers were scheduled to enter kindergarten in 1995, just as Cleveland abolished full-day kindergarten. This change could have influenced parents to take vouchers.

9. There was an additional drop-off of 9 percent in the third-year follow-up test in New York.

10. The fifth- sixth-grade cohort of African Americans, where much of the gain in test scores occurred in New York, is a small proportion of the total African-American sample. Because the difference in test scores between the rest of the African-American sample attending private schools and Latinos attending private schools is probably very low to begin with, explaining an already small difference in test scores with school variable differences is unlikely to produce significant results.

11. An analysis of Chile's national voucher plan, implemented in 1981 and characterized by a large shift in student enrollment from public schools to private voucher schools, showed little, if any, evidence of positive influence on test scores in public schools from increased competition from private schools (McEwan and Carnoy, 2000). This study suggests that, whatever the positive effects of competition on public school test scores, they seem to have been offset by "cream skimming"—the shift of higher-scoring students from public to private schools.

CHAPTER 2

1. Bryk, Lee, and Holland even suggested that many of the characteristics of Catholic high schools could be imported into public education to make it more effective for low-income students.

2. Although this "carries no value judgment," since "all organizations of any size are in some sense bureaucratic" and all government agencies are political, Chubb and Moe claim that the "public school system suffers from very serious problems along both these dimensions. . . . Its bureaucracy problem is not that the system is bureaucratic at all, but that it is too heavily bureaucratic— too hierarchical, too rule-bound, too formalistic—to allow for the kind of autonomy and professionalism schools need if they are to perform well. Its political problem is not that it is subject to any sort of democratic politics, but that the specific political institutions by which the schools are governed actively promote and protect this over-bureaucratization" (p. 26).

3. Their statistical methodology has been sharply criticized elsewhere by Bryk and Lee (1992). First, some of the components used to construct the organizational variables are not organizational properties of the schools, but organizational *consequences;* these, in turn, are correlated with student outcomes, including student achievement. Second, about one-fourth to one-third of the "organizational quality" effect is due to differences in the proportion of students in the academic track. Bryk and Lee argue that this misses the point: academic tracking does not pick up the effect of courses taken by students on their achievement; thus, the variable underestimates the effect of the internal organization of schooling on student performance (see Bryk and Lee, 1992, 444). Chubb and Moe create a third major (unreported) problem when they divide the sample into high- and low-performing schools: the sample weights were not designed for such partitions of the data, potentially seriously biasing the results. A fourth problem is that Chubb and Moe combine reading–vocabulary test score "gains" with math score "gains" in the junior and senior years of high school when, in fact, reading and vocabulary are not taught in high school. So the combined "gain score" measure used is at least in part not a direct outcome of schooling. For another, similar critique, see Cookson (1994, pp. 83–86).

4. Although many of the data used by Chubb and Moe suggest that bureaucracy is particularly onerous in low-income urban areas where school clientele are less-educated parents, they leave out the urban location variable in predicting effective school organization and equivocate on whether parental background affects school autonomy (Bryk and Lee, 1992, p. 447).

5. This is described more fully in a paper by Abelmann and Elmore (1999).

CHAPTER 3

1. Adam Smith and his contemporary Thomas Paine both wrote that education would be much better privately provided.

2. All school and individuals' names have been fictionalized to preserve their anonymity.

3. A recent court decision has prohibited the continuation of the district's quota system for integration; hence United's student profile may have changed since our fieldwork was conducted.

4. Because Olympic Charter School is part of a district that has operated under a federal court desegregation order for nearly two decades, limits are placed on its ability to select students who apply to attend. Students apply for places set aside for children of their racial or ethnic group. The purpose of these quotas is to guarantee a racially integrated school with sufficient numbers of nonminority children to make the school attractive to white families, thus discouraging further white flight from the school district. One teacher estimates that, were it not for Olympic Charter School, most of the white and Korean students would be attending private schools, some of the Latino students would be in parochial schools, but the black students would mostly be attending their neighborhood public schools.

5. Under scrip programs, families purchase tickets that can be redeemed for purchases at local stores. The merchants who agree to accept this scrip then donate a small percentage of these sales to the school.

6. In some states, legislatures have adopted minimal parental participation in school requirements as a condition of receiving welfare benefits, but no state has yet required parents to meet with teachers without making this a condition of benefit eligibility.

Index